The Russian Cookbook

Tatiana M. Maslenikoff

Robert Royal

The Russian Cookbook

Traditional XIX Century Cooking

Candent Ltd. London

Published by Candent Ltd London
72 Fortis Gren Road
Muswell Hill
London N10 3HN
England
Produced by Royal Productions S.L.
Designed by Susi Bilbao
Translated by Jane Walker
Copyright ©Tatiana Ariane Malison
Copyright Photography ©Robert Royal
Printed by V.A. Impresores, S.A. in Spain
UK ISBN: 0-953-77250-0
Legal number: M-4635-2001

To the memory of my father, Mijail Maslenikoff, to whom I owe almost everything I know about Russian cooking, my interest in good food and the sense of the nation of my ancestors.

To my readers with bread, salt, and a glass of vodka, Russians open their doors to friends and to the friends of their friends. Russian hospitality is legendary. As I am unable to open the doors of my own home to everyone, I open those of my restaurant, "El Cosaco" in Madrid, to one and all and offer what I know about Russian cooking.

Table of contents

ntroduction

Just over 30 years ago, my husband and I opened "El Cosaco", the first Russian restaurant in Madrid and, I believe, the first in Spain. Since then we have made many loyal friends who come back time and again to try our dishes.

In this book I have put together many of my favourite recipes; some of them passed on to me by my parents, and others came from old Russian cookery books which I have adapted for modern kitchens.

One of the books which has helped me most in the writing of this one was the first Russian cookery book ever written in Russia where it became very popular. "A Gift to Young Housewives", by Elena Molokhovets, was first published in 1861 and reissued many times until 1917. The book tells the reader how to preserve food and, in general, how to keep a good kitchen and table. For obvious reasons the Soviet government was afraid to publish it after the Revolution.

"A Gift to Young Housewives" is a mine of information about life on a wealthy country estate. The amount of space, number of people and the care needed to feed a family and their dependents at a reasonable standard are almost unimaginable to us today. First one needed an enormous kitchen large enough to take a Russian stove, known as a "pech". It was a huge contraption made of clay or brick, heated with coals, and often weighing more than a ton. As is explained in the chapter on soups, there was no hot plate or cooking surface on a 'pech', and one had to have a second cooker for frying and fast cooking.

Every large household needed to know how to build and care for a "lednik"– an ice house or ice cellar. In Russia ice houses predated by almost 200 years the first ones recorded in England. It would appear that the one in England was built for Charles II in 1660, while in Russia it is documented that in 1482 the Tsar had eleven ice houses to store meat and fish and more than 30 more for storing his drinks.

I remember my father telling me about their cellar in Saratov. He said there was a large entrance from the kitchen which went down into a double cellar.

Before the ice melted in March huge blocks of ice were cut from the Volga River, carried to the house and lowered into a pit in the bottom cellar. The frozen meat and fish were kept on straw-lined shelves in this chamber which had an unpaved floor so the melting ice could drip through to the ground. Preserved fruit and vegetables were kept in the top cellar, some in jars, some in straw and things like sausages, hams or strings of onions hanging from the ceiling. Then there were barrels of salted sauerkraut and the indispensable salted cucumbers, and enough apples and tomatoes to last the family for the rest of the year. They could make ice cream in an ice house of this size, as well as aspics, cold fish, iced vodka and homemade fruit juices.

No wonder that after all the entertaining on their summer estate, and the preparations for the winter my grandmother, Ludmila Leonovska Maslenikova, almost literally collapsed and needed a fortnight in a German spa to recover.

Elena Molokhovets tells us in great detail how to keep grapes for the winter. After meticulous cleaning, each bunch would be put into a clean glass jar, covered with fresh water and sealed. The jars were then stored on a shelf in the cellar and regularly checked one by one to make sure that none of the grapes was going rotten. If they were, the bad one had to be snipped off and the jar resealed.

The amount of labour and space needed for such operations is mind boggling but, according to E.M., it was well worth the effort. She claims that it is impossible to distinguish them from those cut fresh from the vine.

Elena Molokhovets was a Russian Mrs. Beeton. Her book appeared the year serfs were freed, which accounts for unlimited staff in her kitchen. She comments on the illiteracy of servants and tells her readers that instructions on how to perform their duties should be kept simple. She suggests teaching them how to make a broth from scratch as a first step.

In our easy supermarket age it is hard for us to realise how complicated it was for a housewife to plan and organise all the food she would need for many months ahead. In large estates all the cattle, fowl, pigs and rabbits were bred and they had to be slaughtered for storage. She had to work out how many peasants were needed to shoot all the partridge, pheasant and other game for the rest of the year. In her book E.M. describes in detail how to kill a cow and how to butcher a pig. She says that every housewife should learn how it is done even if she prefers not to attend in person. Cleaning out seeds from berries with a hairpin would seem to be a more appropriate job for a lady if she didn't have sufficient help.

What I also found amusing is her advice for keeping and transporting food like live fish. For instance, if you have caught a pike, you should immediately put it in a net and submerge into fresh water. Then take a box the same size as the fish and drill holes into the base and cover it with damp moss. Place a piece of sponge moistened with French wine into the gills of the fish, and set on the moss. Drill holes in the lid and hammer on to top of the box. You can now transport the fish a great distance, but occasionally pour cold water over the box or lower it into a river or lake whenever the opportunity arises. She also gives good advice for "refreshing spoiled grouse", how to keep domestic duck fresh through the winter and many other more practical and easy tips for the housewife.

Elena Molokhovets seems to assume that many young housewives lived in city flats. Although they would probably have had large kitchens by today's standards she had advice for these ladies, just in case. Referring to the sleeping space for the cook, she suggested it be provided by a sturdy wide shelf hinged to the wall. At night the contraption could be lowered, a mattress made from straw or dried seaweed laid on top of it, and folded back against the wall in the morning. In any case, her recipes are helpfully detailed and nearly all the ones I have tested are delicious.

What is Russian cooking? Where does it originate? These two questions are frequently asked by anyone who has travelled through that vast country, or is interested in its customs and its food. There is one simple answer: there is no such thing as a single "Russian cuisine".

Russia is such an enormous country where the climatic regions stretch from the north, with long dark winters, through other more temperate regions, down to the south with its almost Mediterranean weather.

In consequence it is logical that there are many different diets and thus many diverse kinds of food according to the regions. I am referring, of course, to the Russia of my ancestors, which in the 19th Century stretched from the Baltic Sea in the north to the Black Sea in the south, from the Urals in the east to the Carpathians in the west. That was the Russia of the last Tsars. And if we add the cuisine from other federated republics, such as Uzbekistan and Turkmenistan with their varied ethnic and religious influences to that of Russia we have the most diverse of cuisines.

It is not my intention to write an exhaustive study of Russian gastronomy or to reflect on the various regions. My book is basically a collection of the more characteristic recipes of the north (Russia), the centre (Ukraine) and the south (the Caucasus, Georgia and Armenia). All the recipes are for six people, except those which are specifically for a larger number, and those under the heading of 'preserves' which obviously for many more.

The majority of the ingredients are available in larger supermarkets, or in specialised food shops. I hope that my small contribution to the cultural gastronomy of Russia will help to bring a greater understanding between peoples and nations.

Tatiana M. Maslenikoff

From North to South

The cuisine of any country is the fruit of its legends and popular culture. Its geography and climate determine what a nation eats; they make use of the best produce the land and orchards provide. It is one thing eating near the Baltic and quite another doing so on the shores of the Black Sea. Because Russia has such extremes of climate its cuisine runs a whole gamut of possibilities.

People from the great tree-covered plains of the north, where they have long cold winters and short summers, found ways to keep what they had harvested in the summer and autumn to provide food for the winter. They preserved cabbage in brine in large wooden barrels, dried or pickled apples, cucumbers, beef and pork. Wild mushrooms and fungus were threaded on strings to be dried in the sun, fruit was stored with honey and beet sugar. The people learned to make use of their surplus potatoes and wheat to distill into vodka and their dried bread was turned into a very popular low alcohol drink known as 'kvas'.

The food from the northern regions includes thick soups, vegetable or grain purées and pies. Pirogie come in all sizes. They range from pirosyok, those tiny mouthfuls served with borscht, right up to the large kuliebiaka of salmon or other fresh water fish, stuffed with cabbage, wild mushrooms, minced meat and eggs.

In the north they eat soups made from greens and root vegetables combined with meat or fish. The best known soup is borscht, although another soup, schti, has been eaten in Russian homes since time immemorial. It is a soup made up of meat, salt pork and cabbage. There is an old saying which goes: "Schti da kasha pishtia nasha", which can be literally translated as "cabbage soup with kasha keeps us going" –kasha or Saracen grain is like rice in these regions– and another which goes: "Schti da kasha mati nasha", "schti soup and Saracen grains are like our mother to us".

Borscht, like the French cassoulet or any other homemade stew, comes in a thousand-and-one varieties; it differs from one village to another, and every family has its own recipe. Only four ingredients are absolutely essential: cabbage, beetroot, meat or salt pork and sour cream. Everything else depends on what is available and the hands and the pocket of the one who makes it. As we travel further south the cooking becomes more diversified and progressively lighter. Fritters and fried food, such as chicken à la Kiev, or deep fried pirosky make their appearances.

Ukraine is Russia's granary. It was, and still is, the richest region and enjoys the widest variety of agricultural and farm produce. So it comes as no surprise that its cooking is more varied and more sophisticated than that from the north. One example which stands out is 'golubtsy', cabbage and meat rolls. There are also many kinds and shapes of breads from the Ukraine: large, small, round, long, made from many kinds of grain.

In the south —the Caucasus, Georgia and Armenia— the meals are lighter still. There they eat grilled meat —particularly lamb and chicken— green salads, fruit, goat and sheep's cheeses. Wine, olives, rice and yogurt are used for soups, stews and as dressings, Raw or cooked fruits are used in braised meat dishes as well as in desserts.

History and gastronomy

And so Russian cooking adapted itself to its environment. But over the centuries this cuisine has also been enriched by imports from other countries and other cultures. What the world today knows as Russian cooking would be unthinkable without the refinements introduced by the French chefs employed at the courts of the Tsars. The Russian immigrants of 1917, who left for Europe and America, took "Russian cuisine" with them, and when some of them opened Russian restaurants in their places of exile other cultures learned about it and learned to appreciate it. It is an irony of history that at the time the Russian people were suffering starvation and hunger, wars and deprivation, the great restaurants of Paris, London and New York were discovering Russia's ancient culinary art.

Later on we will see that Russian gastronomy is a melting pot of many races and many cultures: the Mongols, the Vikings, the Byzantine Church, Western Europe and others. Invasions, influences and cultural exchanges all brought with them their own ingredients and flavours, and little by little alien habits and traditions injected their particular character into the cooking.

For example, Viking invasions along the Volga and Dnieper Rivers were responsible for the Russian liking for cakes and pastries. They love sweets; in ancient cookery books one can find dozens of recipes for creams, cakes and ice creams. For this they can be grateful to the legendary AsKold, conqueror of Kiev, and to Riurik, who captured Novogrod, Oleg, and other Scandinavian

adventurers. Not only did they sow the seeds of "the Russian State" in the 9th Century, but they also brought with them many delicious dishes such as fruit tarts and the sweet soups made from fresh and dried fruit.

Prince Vladimir I the Great, St. Vladimir and founder of the Russian state, set out to unify the Russian people through religion. He was baptised as a Christian in 989 AD and by marrying the Byzantine Princess Anna Porfirogeneta consolidated the links with Byzantium. In this way he introduced the Christian calendar into Russia, with its days of fasting and abstinence, and the people had to learn to cook without using meat or animal fat. So important is the Church in Russian cooking that I have included a special section on gastronomic customs and typical menus for Post and Pasha (Lent and Easter).

Tea is the national drink of Russia, but it did not originate in Russia. We owe its introduction to the legendary Gengis Khan in 1223, and other Mongol invaders of the 13th and 14th centuries. In the 15th century Ivan the Terrible expelled the Mongols giving rise to the Golden Age, to the growth of large cities, and to the enrichment of the aristocracy and the merchant class. Contacts with other European countries proliferated, and an accumulation of riches gave them the money to acquire more sophisticated objects, and cosmopolitan tastes and habits — not least those of the table. They gave enormous banquets which were still being talked about centuries later.

During the reign of Peter the Great in the 17th Century the European influence penetrated deep into Russian society. Italian and French architects, Dutch shipbuilders, and painters and sculptors from all over Europe arrived in Russia. Rich families brought in great chefs from France, and the names of some of these families —such as the Strogonovs— have gone down in history. The Strogonovs were wealthy merchants who became great financiers, lending money to the Tsars, and generous patrons of the arts. They imported imaginative chefs to cook in their palaces and estates in Ustiori and Solvichegodsk where they created dishes such the universally known "Beef Strogonov". In other noble kitchens French chefs created "Beef Woronov" and "Salade Olivier", which is little more than the Russian salad we know today! Thus, it was the refining influence of French cuisine which gave us what we know as Russian cooking.

Russians are great gourmands. An anecdote told by Nicolai Gogol in his tale "The Drowning" tells it all …

"You don't know what happened to my late mother-in-law," interrupted the farmer. "One night the family were sitting down to supper, my late father-in-law, my mother-in-law, a couple of labourers and their five children. Mother-in-law put some dumplings to cool in a dish. But they were all hungry and couldn't wait until the dumplings had cooled down, so they speared them with their large wooden forks and began to eat. Suddenly a man, whom none of them knew, appeared and asked to be invited to the party. How could they refuse to give food to a hungry man? They gave him a fork and he began to eat the dumplings like a cow eats hay, and soon the bottom of the dish was as smooth as glass, so the mother in law put in some more dumplings. They all thought that their guest would have had his fill and would eat less. But he continued to stuff himself until he had emptied that second dish as well.

"Take care you don't choke on those dumplings," thought my mother-in-law. And suddenly the guest choked and collapsed. They all jumped to his aid, but he was already dead. "Damned glutton! Served him right," she said.

From that moment on my mother-in-law never rested in peace. Every night at dusk the dead man reappeared, sitting over the chimney with a dumpling between his teeth. During the daytime no one mentioned him, but once darkness fell they would look over the hearth, and see him sitting there.

"With a dumpling between his teeth?"
"Yes, with a dumpling between his teeth."

Today, although food and money are scarce one sees a new and timid interest in food in Russia. Over recent years many small family-owned restaurants have opened. When I was in Saratov a couple of years ago the director of the City Museum gave me a new edition of a recipe book of Easter desserts which was first published by local shopkeepers at the beginning of this century. Culture, and especially as in this case, culinary culture, can have its highs and lows, but it is never totally lost.

Beverages

If one had to choose which of the Seven Deadly Sins most characterises the Russian people, one would automatically choose gluttony, and particularly where it concerns drink. Russians drink, they drink a lot, they drink to celebrate, to socialise, to warm themselves, to cool themselves, and above all, to forget.

"Drink is a pleasure for the Russian, they could not live without that pleasure. That is why my people could never convert to Islam which forbids the consumption of alcohol," said St. Vladimir, first Tsar of the Russians, to the Moslem emissaries who had come to offer their religion to the powerful prince when he was searching for a religion to unify his people. At that time the drinks most commonly drunk by the Slavic tribes were kvas and mead. The first is from a fermentation of bread, and the second a fermentation of honey. The distillation of wheat to produce vodka became popular some time later.

Vodkas

The ideal drink to serve with caviar must be vodka, preferably in a bottle frozen into a block of ice. For those who prefer something less strong, a good champagne, sparkling wine, or even a very dry white wine go well with caviar.

The grey-black Russian caviar comes from the sturgeon, or rather from the sturgeon family, of which there are four: beluga, sevruga, osetra and sterlet. With the exception of sterlet, these fish, whose origins go back to prehistoric times, swim up the river Volga from the Caspian Sea. They are fished from the river by fishermen using ancient methods which have been passed down from father to son. The eggs are half-cured in a small quantity of salt. The secret is to use just the right amount of salt to guarantee preservation of the eggs which must be kept at the right temperature. The name "malosol" in Russian means "lightly salted".

Caviar is produced in the following way: the eggs are placed in a strainer and rinsed in fresh water. They are then put in a brine made from approximately 10% salt and packed in small barrels. The quality of the caviar depends basically on the eggs used and the care with which they are treated. It is very important that they are treated immediately they are fished from the water.

The colour and the size of the eggs vary; they can be black, red, grey or golden. The most expensive caviar is the grey or golden caviar from sterlet, the hardest fish to catch. Russia only exports its highest quality caviar, although there are other countries, such as Iran, which produce caviar in smaller quantities.

Sterlet is the only fish of the sturgeon family which never leaves the river; it is smaller than the others, has more delicate flesh and its eggs are a grey-gold in colour. It is the most sought after and almost impossible to obtain. I believe that in the past and up to the dissolution of the Soviet Union it was reserved for high officials in the Kremlin. Beluga caviar, which has the largest eggs, is the second most valued caviar; following that comes sevruga and finally osetra. It is also possible to buy pressed caviar made from crushed eggs. It is like a black paté with a more concentrated flavour and juicy texture than the others. Salmon and trout caviar are also semi-preserved and go wonderfully well with blinis.

Caviar is an essential feature of a good zakusky or hors d'oeuvres, a delicious Russian tradition of which I will talk in greater depth in the next chapter.

Zakusky
and Tapas
Hors D´ouvres

In Western countries zakusky is usually translated as "hors d'oeuvres", but it is not really the correct translation. Zakusky are little tidbits or finger food like those served at cocktail parties. The Spanish "tapas" would be a close equivalent, and Russians, like the Spaniards, are great tapas fans.

In a country where the distances between neighbours were —and still are, in spite of modern transport— so enormous that it was impossible that all the guests would arrive on time at the party, wedding or funeral. And so, centuries ago, there grew up the custom of preparing in the ante-room of a house a large white linen covered table laid out with a wide variety of zakusky, which literally means "mouthful to swallow with a drink." The mouthful, in this case, is usually eaten with a shot of vodka, a wonderful drink to warm up after a long cold sleigh journey. The tradition of the zakusky is widespread across the whole country, with different ingredients according to the region.

I remember with affection and nostalgia the evenings organised by my parents. The preparations began in the morning and I was always brought in as an "assistant" to help with what seemed to my childish eyes as a thousand and one dishes of "heavenly tidbits". Later there was the excitement of the arrival of the guests, all giving the traditional three kisses on the cheek (in memory of the Holy Trinity) bringing flowers for the hostess.

I don't know whether it was the shortage of flowers during the long winter months and the longing for the arrival of Spring but the giving of flowers is of great importance to Russian people. When I visited St. Petersburg a few years ago I was fascinated to see an "open" market, where food was in short supply, but with masses of flowers for sale, brought in every day from the Caucasus by small-time growers, which the people queued up to buy in spite of the high prices. They were perhaps buying a bunch or simply one or two flowers to give as a gift for their hostess.

There were always interminable toasts, with shots of vodka, "na sdarovie", for absent friends, for future joy. And after many glasses had been

consumed it was time for singing, accompanied by a guitar, remembering the great River Volga, "Mother Russia", and romances.

Today, because modern houses are smaller, zakusky are usually served at the table in the dining room as an hors d'oeuvres. It isn't really the same, but nevertheless, better than nothing. A list of typical zakusky could contain the following:

Pickled cucumber	Stuffed vine leaves
Olivier salad	Piroski with meat
Beetroot salad	Piroski with cabbage and egg
Cucumbers in sour cream	Pashtet (homemade paté)
Hard-boiled eggs stuffed with caviar	Herrings in sour cream
Pickled mushrooms	Smoked fish in slices or as canapés
Potato salad á la Russe	Black caviar
Red cabbage salad	Red salmon caviar
Crab and caviar salad	Fresh caviar
Meat balls in tomato sauce	Kazán salad
Poor man's caviar	Cream cheese
Jolodetz (meat in aspic)	Boiled tongue in horseradish sauce
Variety of cold cooked or smoked meat and ham	

Zakusky
Tapas and Hors D'oeuvres

Pickled cucumber, beetroot salad and the ever popular Olivier salad are delicious dishes which form an important part in a selection of hors d'oeuvres. Very few housewives today pickle their own cucumbers, because they need time and space – both of which are in short supply in modern houses. It is a pity because home-pickled cucumbers have a flavour and freshness which tinned ones lack. In many places one can find good quality imported Polish cucumbers, but many of the German cucumbers contain too much vinegar. But I would like to encourage the adventurous cook to experiment and follow the original recipe which I am sure they will enjoy eating.

Russian salad in many varieties and with multiple ingredients, is well known around the world. Unfortunately most of these salads contain little more Russian than the name and the idea. A genuine Russian salad is a Salade Olivier, from the name of the French chef who worked for the Tsars. Like many great salads it contains a little of many things. Every family has its own recipe and I will give you my own without pretending that it is either genuine or the best.

There are many recipes, particularly in the North of Russia, which contain beetroot. One of them is beetroot salad, and I have included a recipe for this as well.

Another recipe is for a Monastery Salad. As the name suggests this has its origins in the monasteries where the Russian orthodox monks lived a strict life never eating meat. Each monastery had a monk who did the cooking, some were better than others, and some used their imagination to create dishes which later became popular outside the monastery walls particularly during Lent. One such dish was a Monastery salad whose basic ingredients are mushrooms and pickled cabbage.

Naturally a good zakusky table must contain caviar, that Russian hors d'oeuvres par excellence. The word caviar actually comes from the Turkish word 'havyar'. In Russia caviar is called 'ikra' and I have already mentioned it in Chapter 3.

I have also included a recipe for herrings, although it these days it is sometimes difficult to find fresh or salted herrings. There are two solutions for this problem: the first is to buy imported German herrings and prepare them with a Russian-style cream. The second way, a little more trouble, is to serve false herrings using decent sized fresh sardines. The advantage of this second method is that it lends itself to various dressings and is actually closer to the original version, and for this reason I have included the second solution.

Kazán, which was capital of the autonomous Tartar republic of the Volga and in whose university studied such people as Tolstoi, Rikov, Lenin and his brother Alexandr Ulianov, has also given its name to a famous salad composed of veal, cucumbers and apples. Kazán Salad is also very nutritious and refreshing.

Salionie Agurtzi
(Pickled cucumbers)

Ingredients

6 glasses cold water

10 cloves

1 tsp black peppercorns

5 bay leaves

1 tbs sugar

3 tbs sugar

2 or 3 sprigs dill

2 doz very small fresh cucumbers

1/2 cup vinegar (Optional – in some regions only salt is used and vinegar is left out)

Fill a large saucepan with water and bring to boil. Scrub the cucumbers and dip into the boiling water for a few seconds and immediately cool under cold running water. This is not to cook, but merely to disinfect them.

Put pickling ingredients and cold water into another large pan and bring to the boil. Take off the heat and leave to cool. Place cucumbers upright in tall glass jars. Pour pickling liquid over cucumbers, seal and keep in a cold place for several weeks.

In Russia the cucumbers are stored in wooden barrels in caves and cellars and will last throughout the winter.

Olivier Salad

Ingredients

2 cooked chicken breasts

2 large potatoes cooked in their skins

3 hard-boiled eggs

1/2 cup / 4 fl oz / 112 ml.) sour cream

3/4 cup / 6 fl oz / 170 ml)
homemade mayonnaise

2 tbs chopped capers

3 cooked carrots

2 small cooked turnips

1 cup cooked peas

100 g / 4 oz cooked ham

1 tsp chopped dill

1 tsp salt

1/4 tsp ground white pepper

Peel cold boiled potatoes. Finely dice potatoes, carrots, turnips, chicken, boiled ham and hard-boiled eggs. Mix the mayonnaise with the sour cream and capers. Reserve a little to decorate the salad and add the remainder to other ingredients. Pile up the salad on a bed of lettuce leaves on a large round platter. Smooth and cover with remaining mayonnaise. Decorate with capers, hard boiled eggs, radishes etc.

Gribi v Smetane
(Oyster mushrooms with sour cream)

Ingredients

1 k/ 2 1/4 lb oyster mushrooms
(fresh or tinned)

1 onion

2 cloves garlic

4 tbs butter

1 tsp dill

1/2 tsp salt

1/4 tsp pepper

1 tbs flour

8 fl. oz/1 cup sour cream

4 fl. oz/1/2 cup milk

2 tbs Worcester sauce

If using fresh mushrooms, slice and wash in plenty of cold water. Blanch briefly in salted water and leave to drain.

Finely chop onion and garlic. Melt butter in a large frying pan, add onions and garlic and fry gently for about 5 minutes. Add the flour and stir until mixed. Pour in milk, sour cream, dill and Worcester sauce and cook over moderate heat until cooked and thickened.

Fold mushrooms into sour cream sauce. Serve on toasted bread as a first course.

Kartofelni Salat
(Potato salad)

Ingredients

5 potatoes boiled in their skins

2 spring onions

1 cup chopped pickled herrings

2 hard boiled eggs

1/4 cup capers or half capers and
half dill pickles

Dressing

1/2 cup sunflower oil

2 tbs vinegar

1 tsp sugar

1 tsp mustard

1/4 cup water

1 tsp dill

1 tsp chopped parsley pinch pepper

1/2 tsp salt

Peel and boil potatoes and cut into medium slices while still warm. Chop spring onions and mix with remaining ingredients.

Mix all dressing ingredients together and pour over the salad. Stir well and leave to rest in the fridge for a couple of hours. Dress the salad while the potatoes are still warm.

Salat iz Kracni Kapusti
(Red cabbage salad)

Ingredients

1 small or 1/2 large red
cabbage

2 medium onions

4 carrots

2 sour apples

Dressing

1/4 cup vinegar

1/2 cup water

4 tbs olive oil

1 tsp sugar

1/2 tsp salt

1/4 tsp pepper pinch ground clove

Shred cabbage as fine as possible. Finely slice onions and grate carrots and apple.

Mix dressing ingredients together and add to salad. Leave to rest in the fridge a couple of hours.

Salat iz Craba c Ikroi
(Crab salad with red caviar)

Ingredients

1 large green apple

1 lb / 1/2 k white crab meat

(can be tinned)

1 cooked potato

1 dill-pickled cucumber

1/2 cup cocktail sauce

6 crisp lettuce leaves

2 lemons

1 tomato

6 tsp salmon caviar

Chop apple, cooked potato and cucumber as finely as possible. Mix with crab meat and cocktail sauce.

Place a lettuce leaf on each plate and divide a portion of crab salad on each of them. Sprinkle caviar over each individual salad and decorate with slices of lemon and tomato.

Tiftieli v Tomatnom Sousom
(Mini meat balls in tomato sauce)

Ingredients

1/2 k/ 1 lb minced veal

1/4 k/ 8 oz minced pork

3 slices crumbled white bread

2 eggs

1 cup cold milk

1 medium-sized onion grated

1/2 tsp salt

1/4 tsp pepper flour oil for frying

Sauce

1/2 k/ 1 lb passata

1 cup sour cream

2 tbs soy sauce few drops tabasco

Beat the eggs with milk, salt, pepper and breadcrumbs. Add minced meat and grated onion. Shape into balls the size of large olives. Flour and then fry in hot oil until golden.

Mix ingredients for sauce and warm over a low heat. Serve meat balls in a dish with the sauce separately.

Baklajanaia Ikra
(Aubergine or poor man's caviar)

Ingredients

3 medium aubergines

1 large clove garlic

1 tsp chopped parsley

1 peeled tomato (optional)

1/2 onion finely chopped

1/2 cup olive oil

3 tbs lemon juice salt and pepper

to taste

Roast aubergines in moderate oven until soft. Cool slightly and then peel. Purée all the ingredients together in a food processor, not too fine. It should remain slightly lumpy.

Leave to rest several hours and serve in a bowl surrounded by white and brown thin toast.

Holodiets
(Cold meat in aspic)

Ingredients

1 k / 2 1/4 lb stewing veal in
one piece

1 calf's foot

3 peeled carrots

2 peeled onions

2 bay leaves

2 stalks celery

10 black peppercorns

1 tsp salt

1 pickled cucumber

1 fresh cucumber

1 litre / 1 3/4 pt water

Sauce

1/2 cup grated horseradish

1 cup sour cream

1/4 tsp salt

1/2 tsp sugar

(1 1/2 litre / 2 1/2 pt capacity loaf tin)

Put all ingredients, except cucumbers, in a pressure cooker in a litre of water. Cook for 35 minutes and leave to cool. In a regular pot, allow two hours for cooking.

Separate the meat and the gelatinous part of the calf's foot from the bones. Cut all the meat into chunks about 2 cm or 1 inch. Clarify the stock and cool in the fridge. When it begins to set put a small amount on the bottom of the loaf tin or in individual ramekins. Decorate the base with slices of carrots and fresh and pickled cucumbers. Fill the moulds or ramekins with the chunks of meat and then top up with the remaining stock and cucumbers. Refrigerate until time to serve.

Mix all the ingredients for horseradish sauce and serve separately.

Dolmas
Stuffed vine leaves

Dolmas
(Stuffed vine leaves)

Ingredients

1 jar vine leaves

1/2 k / 1 lb minced veal or lamb
or half of each

2 cups cooked rice

1 cup finely chopped chives, parsley
and dill

1/2 cup currants

1/4 tsp grated nutmeg and cinnamon

1/2 tsp salt

1/4 tsp pepper

To cook

1/2 cup lemon juice

1/2 cup olive oil

1 cup water

Separate and rinse vine leaves and lay out on the work surface. Cut out the stalks.

Mix stuffing ingredients in a bowl. Place a spoonful of stuffing on each leaf, fold in sides and roll into a small sausage.

Place in a pan, preferably cast iron, in several layers. Cover with cooking liquid. Cover pan as tightly as possible and cook over a low heat 40 minutes.

(These can be made without meat, and in this case increase the amount of rice. This is a very popular dish in many regions of Russia, particularly near the Caspian and Eastern Mediterranean. They are eaten cold or warm and the stuffing varies according to the region and religion).

Preserved vine leaves

As vine leaves keep very well, it is a good idea
to preserve them by the dozen and keep
them in a cool place for future use.

These are best made in the spring when the
leaves are fully out but still young and tender.
Cut a good sized bunch of vine leaves and
wash them well. Put in a pan, cover with
water , salt and a few spoonfuls of vinegar.
(The amount depends on the quantity of leaves and
water.) Bring them to the boil and immediately
remove from the heat. When they have cooled
slightly, remove from the water and roll up a bunch
of leaves and place them in tall glass jars. Pour over
the cooking liquid. Seal and sterilize immediately.
These should keep for up to one year.

Preserved vine leaves can be purchased in
specialized Mediterranean food stores.

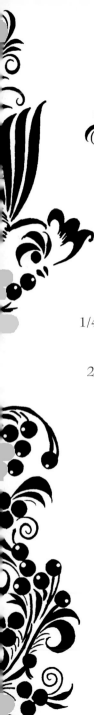

Piroski
(Mini meat pasties)

Ingredients

1k / 2 1/4 lb ready-made
puff pastry

1/2 k / 1 lb minced veal

1/4 k / 1/2 lb good quality sausage
meat

200 g / 6 oz chopped mushrooms

1 finely chopped large onion

1/2 tsp salt

1/4 tsp ground pepper

1 egg yolk

2 tbs corn or sunflower oil

Fry onions and mushroom in oil. When golden add meat, season and stir. The meat should remain slightly underdone to keep the piroski juicy.

Roll out pastry on a floured board to thickness of 30 mm. Cut into rounds with a glass or pastry cutter.

Arrange small spoonfuls of stuffing on each pastry disc. Fold pastry over in half-moon shapes and seal well. Place, seam side down, on an oven sheet. Glaze with egg yolk diluted with a little water. Cook in hot oven for around 20 minutes or until cooked.

Piroski with Cabbage and Egg

Ingredients

1 finely chopped large onion

6 cups shredded cabbage

3 hard boiled eggs

1/2 tsp salt

1/4 tsp ground pepper

16 fl. oz / 2 cups chicken stock

2 tbs corn or sunflower oil

1 k / 2 1/4 lb puff pastry

Fry onion in a little oil, add cabbage, chicken stock, season with salt and pepper. Cover and cook over moderate heat for 20 minutes. Put in a bowl and add chopped hard-boiled egg. Allow to cool before filling piroski.

Roll out pastry on floured board to thickness of 30 mm. Cut into rounds with a glass or pastry cutter.

Arrange small spoonfuls of stuffing on each pastry disc. Fold over in half-moon shapes and seal well. Place, seam side down on an oven sheet. Glaze with egg yolk diluted with a little water. Cook in hot oven 15-20 minutes, or until cooked.

Piroski can also be stuffed with fromage frais seasoned with salt, pepper and chopped dill weed. A plainer version of piroski can be made with the dough used for pirogui. (See page 139).

Paschtet
(Liver pate)

Ingredients

1/2 k / 1 lb chicken livers
1/4 k / 1/2 lb calves liver
1/2 onion finely chopped
10 tbs butter
1/2 cup grated parmesan cheese
1/4 tbs ground pepper
1/4 tbs salt
1 glass brandy

Clean chicken livers of fat and any fibres. Blanch briefly in boiling salted water. Brown chopped onions in half the butter, add chicken and calves liver cut into chunks and briefly cook, leaving the meat underdone . Pour over the brandy and flame.

Remove from the heat and add the remaining butter and grated cheese. Purée in food processor or blender. Pour into serving dish and refrigerate for several hours.

Sielodka po Ruski
(Russian-Style pickled herrings)

Ingredients

2 k / 4 1/2 lb fresh herring fillets
(or large sardines)
1 k / 2 1/4 lb coarse salt
Cold weak tea

Dressing n.° 1

Vegetable or olive oil
Finely sliced sweet onion
Ground pepper
A few bay leaves

Dressing n.° 2

Sour cream
Finely sliced sweet onion
Dill weed

Wash herring fillets and remove small bones. Pour a layer of salt in a glass or earthenware dish. Place a layer of herring on the salt, folding them over if they are large. Cover with a second layer of salt. Continue layering fish and salt until all herrings are used. Complete with a final layer of salt. Cover and leave in the fridge 4 or 5 days. Remove from salt and wash in cold running water. Leave to soak overnight in cold tea. When ready to serve remove the skin and any bones which remain. The fish are now ready to finish in the dressing of your choice.

Dressing n.° 1: Place fish fillets in a flat dish with a layer of onion, pepper and whole bay leaves on top. Cover with a layer of oil. Leave to infuse for several hours before serving.

Dressing n.° 2: Place fish fillets in a flat dish. Cover with a layer of sour cream, sliced onion and chopped dill. Leave to infuse for several hours before serving.

(No measurements are given for the dressings. The quantity depends on the number of fish fillets.)

Svezaia Ikra
(Fish roe caviar)

Ingredients

2 whole large salmon
or trout roe

1 tsp salt

2 tbs vegetable oil

1 tbs lemon juice

1 cup finely chopped spring onion

Sour cream

Skin the fish roe and pour 1/2 litre boiling water over them. Drain immediately and place in a glass dish. Mix in the remaining ingredients, except the sour cream. Cover with cling wrap and leave in the refrigerator overnight. Serve with sour cream in a separate dish.

67

Farsherovanaye Iatze c Ikroi
(Stuffed eggs with caviar)

Ingredients

6 hard-boiled eggs

2 tbs finely chopped spring onions
or chives

1 tsp chopped dill weed

1/2 cup tartar sauce

2 tbs black caviar

2 tbs salmon caviar

Cut eggs in half, remove yolks and sieve into a bowl. Add tartar sauce, spring onions and dill weed and mix together. Stuff the mixture into egg whites and scatter red caviar over 6 of the whites and black caviar over the remainder.

To prevent the serving dish turning black from the cooked eggs, place a white napkin or a layer of chopped lettuce on the plate before arranging the eggs.

Pashtet iz Cira
(Russian cheese spread)

Ingredients

1/4 k / 8 oz cream cheese
1/4 tsp garlic salt
1 pinch ground white pepper
1/2 cup finely chopped walnuts

Mix ingredients together and form into a ball shape. Decorate with walnut halves. Serve with thinly sliced brown or black bread.

Jazik c Hrenom
(Boiled tongue with horseradish sauce)

Ingredients

1 calf tongue

1 k / 2 1/4 lb coarse salt

1 tbs fine salt

1 tbs sugar

3/4 cup saltpetre

2 carrots

1 onion

2 leeks

2 bay leaves

1 tsp black peppercorns bouquet garni of thyme, parsley and rosemary

4 oz thinly sliced bacon

Horseradish sauce n.° 1:
Mix 1/2 cup grated horseradish with 1/2 cup sour cream

Horseradish sauce n.° 2:
Mix 1/2 cup grated horseradish with 1/2 cup finely chopped beetroot cooked in vinegar

Clean tongue, cover with cold water and leave to soak for 3 hours. Remove from water and dry with a clean cloth. Pierce the tongue in several places with a skewer. Mix saltpetre with fine salt and sugar and rub this mixture well into the tongue. Leave to rest in the refrigerator for 1 hour.

Cover the bottom of a long earthenware or stainless steel dish with one quarter of the coarse salt. Put tongue on the salt and cover with the remainder. Cover and put in the refrigerator for a week turning it every two days with two wooden spoons. (Do not touch with your hands).

After a week remove the tongue from the salt, wash and leave to soak in cold water overnight. The following day boil the tongue in a large pan in plenty of water for 10 minutes and then change the water. Return tongue to the saucepan, cover once more with more water, the herbs and vegetables. Bring to the boil and cook for approximately 3 hours in a normal pan or 1 1/2 hours in a pressure cooker.

Peel the tongue while still warm and wrap in the thinly sliced bacon. Wrap in a clean cloth. It will keep for up to a week in the fridge. Slice into thin slices and serve with horseradish sauce.

Rozdestvo
a Christmas Menu

Russians celebrate Christmas on January 7th – December 25th in the Russian Orthodox Julian calendar. In Russia, as in almost all Christian countries, Christmas is a family affair with the children at the centre of the party. The Christmas tree –iolka– is decorated with sweets, coloured birds and candles, and the traditional gifts are brought by "Dedushka Maroz" (Grandpa Frost) an old grandfather figure with a long snowy-white beard and dressed in a white sparkling suit.

In olden times it was the custom to fast until sunset of December 24th, and in the evening, while the family was decorating the tree, they ate "kutia", a special rice or wheat dish cooked with fruit and nuts. As night fell Dedushka Maroz arrived bringing presents for the children while everyone danced around the Christmas tree and sang traditional songs. And then they sat down to dinner. These customs still survive today, although during the Soviet times, instead of Dedushka Maroz, it was the postman who brought the gifts. December 25th was taken up with visiting family and friends, with children's parties at tea time.

Many Russian authors wrote about the gastronomic Christmas feasts in their stories and novels. Nicolai Gogol wrote a book called simply "Christmas Eve", a story about witches, devils and stealing the moon on dark nights, but where "kutia" played an important role.

"Chub, the rich Cossack, had been invited by the deacon to eat kutia with him on Christmas Eve. He had also invited the Mayor, a relative of the deacon —who wore a blue frock coat and sang in a deep base voice in the Archbishop's chapel— the Cossack Sverbigus and several other guests. In addition to the kutia they drank saffron 'eau de vie', eating "varanez " and many other dishes."

Nicolai Gogol also wrote: "While the young people went to find their sleigh, the thin old gossip came out of the inn in a bad mood after they had refused to give him any more on credit. He had hoped to stay there a while to see if some generous nobleman would come in and buy him a drink. But it was

as if they had all reached an agreement and no one arrived. They were all good Christians and were still at home eating "kutia" with their families. He walked along the road, musing on the way customs had become corrupted and on the insensitive heart of the Jewess who sold the wine, when he tripped over the sacks. He stopped and stared at them in astonishment.

"Look at the sacks someone has left in the road," he said to himself looking around him. "I'm sure they contain chunks of meat. Aren't I lucky to find such enormous sacks! It would be good for me if they were full of cakes and grechaniki." – although there was only bread."

A Christmas Menu

Christmas menus vary in different regions and according to family traditions. The one that follows is one of many; it is as traditional to serve goose as it is to serve duck or ham. Hvorost (branches), the Christmas dessert, is a fried dough sprinkled with icing sugar to look like dried snowy branches in the woods. It is also traditional to put out a tray of sweets with nuts, sugared almonds, mandarines and tropical fruit.

A typical Christmas menu:

Smoked salmon garnished with hard boiled eggs, finely chopped onions,
capers and parsley
Meat and mushroom stuffed piroski
Olivier salad
Hard-boiled eggs stuffed with red and black caviar
Cold tongue with horseradish sauce
Beetroot and walnut salad
Served with vodka

Roast goose stuffed with apples
Potatoes sautéed in goose fat
Glazed onions
Served with red wine

Hvorost and winter fruit compote
Served with dry champagne or sparkling wine

Silver tray of sweetmeats and fruit
Served with semi sweet champagne or sparkling wine

Kutiá

Ingredients

1 cup / 200g / 7 oz poppy seeds

2 cups / 400g / 14 oz wheat or oats

1/2 tsp salt

4 tbs honey

3 tbs currants or raisins

3 tbs chipped almonds

1 1/2 l. / 1 1/4 pts water

Raspberries or glacé cherries

Cover poppy seeds with cold water and leave to soak overnight. Drain in a sieve. Rinse the wheat or oats with boiling water. Bring 1 1/2 litres of water to the boil, add the salt and the grain. Bring back to the boil, cover and put in a moderate oven for 4 hours (30 mins at maximum in a microwave). Drain the poppy seeds and crush them in a morter or electric blender. Add to the cooked wheat. In a cup of water (or almond milk) mix together the honey, currants and almonds. Pour the mixture over the wheat.

Serve in mounds on a tray, decorated with cherries or raspberries. The tray is usually presented on a bed of straw as a symbol of the birth of Jesus Christ.

Gus Farcherovanoia c Iblokami
(Goose stuffed with apples)

Ingredients

1 5k / 12 lb plump goose

4 green apples

1 tsp salt

1/2 tsp ground pepper

1/2 cups / 100g / 7 oz currants or raisin

pinch dried marjoram

Remove all visible fat from the cavity of the goose. Wash and dry well. Season inside and outside the bird with salt and pepper.

Peel, core and quarter the apples. Stuff the goose with the apples, the raisins and marjoram. Sew or skewer the cavity closed. Lightly grease the skin with some of the goose fat. Roast in a 200 C / 400 F oven for half the cooking time. Reduce to 170 C / 325 F and cook until the bird is cooked. Leave to rest 15 minutes in a warm place before carving.

(The cooking time will depend on the weight of the bird. Allow about 40 minutes per kilo/20 minutes per lb).

Hvorost
(Fritters)

Ingredients

4 egg yolks

1/3 cup / 3 fl oz double cream

1/4 cup / 2 fl oz brandy

1 1/2 tsp icing sugar

1 1/2 cups / 7 oz / 210 g flour

3 cups sunflower oil

Icing sugar to decorate

Mix the first five ingredients together and knead well. Roll out as thin as possible on a floured marble slab. Cut into 8 x 3 cm(3 x 1 1/2 ins) strips. Make a small incision at one end of each strip and fold the other end through the cut. Fry in plenty of hot oil and sprinkle with icing sugar.

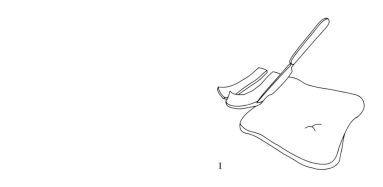

1

2

 Post i Pasha
Lent and Easter

Christian practices, imported in the 10th Century from the Byzantine Empire, combine with pagan traditions at holiday times in Russia.

When the first signs of the thaw appeared after a long dark winter, northern tribes awoke from their lethargy to celebrate Festival of the Sun. They made little round pancakes to offer as gifts to the Sun God so he would not forget to warm up Mother Earth, and she in turn would make the crops sprout. They ate these little pancakes –blini– with butter, fish and dried meat. According to historians and archeologists, the Festival of the Sun was celebrated in fancy dress and with the burning of a dummy of "The Prince of Winter".

With the coming of Christianity to Russia, the Spring Festival coincided with the start of Lent, 40 days before the Resurrection of Christ. They celebrated Maslinitza (Butter Cake Festival) with a great eating binge when blini were eaten with smoked fish, herrings or caviar, but never meat. At end of the three days of the Maslinitza, the strict fasting of Lent began in earnest.

Russian Lent is divided into Lent and Greater Lent. During the first period one can eat anything except meat or fowl; in the second part no animal products of any kind are permitted. This forbids even eggs, butter and milk, and a housewife must use all her imagination to think of appetising meals for the family – particularly since fruit and vegetables are still scarce at this time of the year in the cold northern latitudes. Meals in most households must have been a genuine penance.

My father told me that even white sugar was forbidden in his grandfather's house because animal bones were used to make the charcoal to refine the sugar, and so during Lent only cubes of unrefined brown sugar cut by hand were served. The only ones happy with these sugar lumps were the children who ate them as sweets.

Monastirski Salat
(Monastery salad)

Ingredients

1 cup / 225g/8 oz pickled
cabbage
1/2 k / 1 lb boletus
2 pickled cucumbers
3 boiled potatoes
1 cup / 225g/8 oz stoned black olives
1 small onion
Lettuce leaves to garnish
1/2 litre/3/4 pt court bouillon

Dressing

1/4 cup olive oil
3 tbs cider or white wine vinegar
1 tsp chopped dill weed
1/2 tsp sugar
1/4 tsp salt
pinch of pepper
1 clove of garlic lightly crushed

Bring court bouillon to the boil and briefly blanch the boletus. Drain and chill.

Several hours before serving, prepare the dressing by mixing all ingredients together. Remove the crushed garlic shortly before using. Pour the dressing over the drained boletus and leave to stand in the refrigerator for several hours.

Arrange a few lettuce leaves on the serving dish. Finely chop onions, cut cucumbers in slices. Peel potatoes and slice. Mix boletus with the cabbage, olives, cucumber and onions. Arrange the potatoes on the lettuce and finally pour the salad dressing over them.

Blini

Blini iz Tri Mouki
(Three flour blini)

Ingredients

3 eggs

2 cups / 280g / 10 oz plain flour

1 cup / 140g / 5 oz mixed rye and
buckwheat flour

2 tsp bakers yeast

3/4 l / 1/4 pt tepid milk

1/4 l / 1/2 pint tepid water

1/2 tsp salt

1 tsp sugar

4 tbs melted butter

lump of lard to grease pan

(The quantity of milk and water is only
approximate. Some flours absorb liquid
more than others. The batter should
not be too liquid)

Dissolve the yeast and sugar in the tepid water. Mix the three flours with the milk and beat until the batter is smooth and then gradually beat in the yeast and water and continue beating. Leave to prove in a warm place, covered with a clean cloth, for about 2 hours. Separate the eggs and put the whites to one side. Add the yolks to the dough with the butter and salt. Beat for 2 minutes. Leave to prove for a further hour, or until it has tripled in volume. When ready to fry the blini, whip the egg whites until stiff and fold into the dough.

Heat a couple of small heavy frying pans and grease with a little lard. Pour about 2 tbs of the batter into each pan and spread out using a circular motion. Turn each blini when the surface is pitted with small holes. Cover with a clean cloth and keep warm in a cool oven. Serve with melted butter, sour cream and a variety of smoked fish, herrings and caviar.

Krasnoie Blini
(Fine blini)

Ingredients

2 1/2 cups / 350g / 12 oz flour

2 1/2 cups / 20 fl oz milk

2 eggs (separated)

2 tbs melted butter

1/2 tbs sugar

1/2 tsp salt

1 tbs bakers yeast

(The quantity of milk is only approximate.
Some flours absorb more liquid than others.
The final result should not be too runny)

Warm the milk to blood temperature keeping one cupful separate. In a large bowl mix the remaining milk with the yeast and the flour. Beat for about 3 minutes and leave to rise in a warm place, away from draughts, for about 1 1/2 hours. Mix together the remaining cup of milk with the egg yolks, melted butter, the sugar and salt. When the dough has doubled in volume add the milk and egg mixture beating well. Leave to rise for another hour. Beat the egg whites until stiff and add to the dough just before cooking the blini.

Grease and heat two 15 cm/6 inch griddle or non-stick frying pans. Pour about 1 1/2 tbs of the batter to each one and move the pan around in a circular motion until the batter covers the whole pan. When one side is golden brown, turn over and brown the other side. Turn out and cover with a clean cloth keeping them warm in a cool oven. Continue making blini until all the dough is used up. Serve with sour cream, melted butter and smoked fish or caviar.

Kartofelnie Kotlety c Gribnom Sousom
(Potato cakes with mushroom sauce)

Ingredients

6 large potatoes

3 egg yolks

1/4 cup / 35g / 1 1/2 oz flour

3/4 cup / 100g / 4 oz breadcrumbs

1/2 tsp white pepper

1/2 cup / 112 ml / 4 fl oz vegetable oil

1/2 tsp salt

12 mushrooms

1 tbs butter

24 leaves parsley

Sauce

8 dried mushrooms

1 tbs butter

1/2 finely chopped onion

1/2 tsp salt

1/4 tsp white pepper

1 tbs sour cream

Peel the potatoes and cook in abundant boiling water until soft. Pass them through a sieve while still warm. Beat the egg yolks and gradually add them to the potatoes along with the flour, salt and white pepper. Beat the dough with a wooden spoon until smooth and fluffy. Form the dough into 12 oval shapes and roll them in breadcrumbs, pressing in well.

Heat the oil in a frying pan and fry the potato cakes in batches of three for about 2 minutes each side. Meanwhile fry the mushroom caps in butter until golden. Decorate each potato cake with a mushroom and parsley leaf.

Mushroom sauce

Soak the mushrooms in 2 cups of hot water for about 20 minutes and then simmer over medium heat for another 20 minutes. Melt the butter and lightly brown the onion, add the flour and stir with a wooden spoon gradually adding 1 cup of the strained mushroom water. If the sauce is too thick add a little more of the mushroom liquid, salt and pepper. Chop the mushrooms and add to the sauce. Remove from the heat and add the sour cream.

Blinchitei Pirog
Blini Cake

Blinchitei Pirog
(Blini Cake)

Ingredients

1 k / 2 1/4 lb flaky pastry

2 x 30 cm /12 in blini

2 cups white sauce

1 egg yolk

Filling 1

300 g / 9 oz cooked and sliced
mushrooms
1 chopped onion browned in oil

Filling 2

6 finely sliced cooked carrots

Filling 3

1 cup cooked rice
2 chopped hard boiled eggs

Divide the white sauce into three separate bowls. Mix one portion of the filling into each bowl. Taste and season with salt and pepper if needed.

Roll out one third of the pastry into a circle of about 40 cms / 16 inches in diameter. Heap the first filling into the centre of the pastry leaving a rim of about 5 cms / 2 inches all round. Cover with one of the blini and place the second filling on top. Cover with the second blini and then add with the third filling. Roll out the remaining 2/3 of the pastry and drape over the top of the fillings. Cut off any excess pastry and seal the edges with the egg yolk. Cut a small hole in the centre for the steam to escape and paint the surface with the remaining egg yolk.

Cook in a preheated hot oven for about 35 minutes or until golden.

Serve with a small cup of vegetable broth. Sometimes a fourth layer of stuffing is added, using chopped cooked spinach mixed with white sauce.

Kabachok Farshirovani c Ovaschami
(Stuffed courgettes)

Ingredients

3 large courgettes

1/2 cup chopped onion

3 tbs butter

1 cup cooked chopped carrots

1 cup cooked chopped potatoes

1/2 cup cooked chopped turnips

1 tsp salt

1/4 tsp ground pepper

2 tbs grated cheese

2 cups white sauce

1 tsp dill weed

Heat the oven to 180 C / 350 F. Fry the onion in the butter until lightly browned, add the turnip, carrot and potatoes. Remove from the heat and season with salt and pepper.

Cut the courgettes into 8 cm/3 1/2 inch slices and empty out most of the flesh without cutting right through to the base, reserving the flesh. Cover with plenty of salted water and cook for about 5 minutes. Remove from the water and plunge into a bowl of iced water to stop the cooking. Place, open side up, in a greased oven proof dish.

Chop the courgette flesh and fry in a little butter for a few minutes, add the remaining vegetables and season with salt and pepper. Fill the courgette cups, sprinkle with grated cheese and cook in the oven for about 20 minutes. Add chopped dill weed to the white sauce and serve separately.

As his weeping died down Garaska got to his feet and showed the guard his right hand, sticky with a yellow and white mess. Bargamot, who still didn't understand what was going on, thought something really sad had happened.

"I wanted to greet you... on the Resurrection of Christ.... to give you an egg, and you..."

Bargamot was moved; poor Garaska had greeted him with the noble and Christian intention of giving him the three kisses and an egg, and he had detained him.

"Heavens above, man!" he exclaimed shaking his head.

He felt annoyed with himself, his behaviour with his brother in Christ had been truly cruel.

"I'm sorry, man. I am a Christian too," he mumbled.

And he leaned over to the drunk, scraping his sabre on the ground.

"So you've broken your egg then?"

"I've made mincemeat of it....I wanted to greet you...I'm a good Christian....and you wanted to take me to the police station...."

The guard's remorse was greater every minute.

"Come home with me," he said in a determined voice. "You shall eat with us."

And the tale continues in the spirit of Easter....

"Ivan Akindinich, when are you going to give Vania the Easter egg?" his wife asked the guard.

"Later, later....there's no hurry," he replied.

"Help yourself to more soup," said Maria, passing the bowl to Garaska. "Help yourself to more soup, Guerasim...I don't know your patronymic."

"Andreich,"

"Help yourself to more soup, Guerasim Andreich," she said.

Garaska choked on the mouthful he was about to swallow. He dropped the spoon and lay his head on the table. He began to moan, as he had done half an hour earlier when he had so upset Bargamot. The children were scared when they heard him and they too dropped their spoons and started to cry. Bargamot looked across at his wife with concern.

"Why are you crying, Guerasim Andreich?" she asked him both kindly and affectionately.

"You called me by both my names," mumbled the drunk, still snivelling. "It is the first time since the day I was born that anyone called me by both names...."

This story, by Leonidas Andreiev, is called "Bargamot and Goraski". It is rather sad, although really there is nothing more cheerful than a Russian Easter.

We have come back from church. The Easter table is laid, and it is like a spring song. The many dishes, a thousand and one varieties of salad, traditional sweets garnished with flowers and coloured eggs appear to spring out of the snow of the white linen table cloth. It is like a work of art or the magic of some northern fairy who has woven her spell.

The midnight supper is traditionally a cold buffet, with perhaps one or two hot dishes. Around the table the family congregate with old friends and long lost friends who they have met outside the church. The children, who have had a long afternoon nap, are full of energy and running around delighted to be with the grown ups until all hours and to be wearing new clothes.

A typical Easter dinner could include:

Roast or boiled ham

Beetroot salad

Hot or cold stuffed suckling pig, either roast or boiled

Green salad

Rolled lamb or roast chicken in aspic

Pickled cucumbers

Salade Olivier

Marinated muchrooms

Pasha and kulich surrounded by coloured eggs

Paracionek c Gelé
(Suckling pig in aspic)

Ingredients

1 5 k / 12 lb suckling pig,
partboned with the head and
legs intact
1 fine muslin cloth
2 carrots
2 sticks celery
2 leeks
1 bouquet garni
1 onion
10 grains peppercorns
3 tsp salt
4 cloves
4 bay leaves
2 cloves garlic
6 sheets gelatine
1 glass dry sherry

Garnish

1 bunch watercress
1 apple

Sauces

1 jar horseradish
2 cups sour cream
1/2 k / 1 lb apple sauce

Tie the feet neatly underneath the belly of the pig and wrap in the muslin cloth. Place it in a large fish-kettle, belly side down, and cover with cold water, add all remaining ingredients except the gelatine and sherry.

Cover and place on the heat. When it begins to boil reduce the heat to medium and simmer for about 1 1/2 hours – test with a skewer which should go in easily. Cool in the cooking liquid and remove the muslin.

Clarify the broth and use 1/2 litre to dissolve the gelatine adding the glass of sherry. Cool slightly and when it begins to gel paint the pig with several layers of the jelly using a pastry brush. Place on a platter with the apple in its mouth and garnish with the remainder of the jelly chopped into dice and surround with the watercress. To add a little colour a few slices of carrot or cherries can be used. Serve with the horseradish or apple sauce. Carve the pig into slices like a sausage.

Roulad iz Barachka
(Stuffed lamb)

Ingredients

1 large boned leg of lamb

1 large chopped onion

100 gr / 4 oz dried mushrooms

100gr / 4 oz cooked buckwheat or

wild rice

2 bay leaves

1 tsp salt

1/2 tsp pepper

1 tbs corn oil

1 bouquet garni

Salt and pepper

Make a stock using the lamb bones, bouquet garni, salt and pepper. Put the mushrooms to soak in very hot water for 3 hours.

Fry the finely chopped onion in the oil until they are golden, add the chopped mushrooms, season and mix with the buckwheat or rice. Stir and remove from the heat. Open out the leg of lamb and flatten slightly with a meat hammer. Use the stuffing to fill the lamb and sew it up securely.

Pour a little oil and bay leaves onto the base of an earthenware dish and seal the lamb on all sides. Roast for 1 1/2 hours basting occasionally with the stock. Serve very hot garnished with glazed shallots and carrots.

Zharinaia Vichiná
(Roast leg of pork)

Ingredients

4-6 k / 9-12 lb leg of pork boned

100 g salt

10 peppercorns

3 bay leaves

6 cloves

5 cloves garlic

2 glasses white wine

Preparation should begin two days before serving. Fill a large pan with salted water and when it comes to the boil submerge the pork in the water and bring back to the boil. Immediately remove the meat from the water and place in a large glass or china bowl. Bring to the boil a generous 3 litres of water, the salt, bay leaves, peppercorns, cloves and garlic. Pour over the meat. Cover and refrigerate for 2 days turning every 12 hours.

Remove the meat from the brine and dry well with clean cloths. Tie the meat with string to keep its shape while cooking. Roast the meat in a moderate oven for 40 minutes per kilo. Serve hot or cold. If hot, the traditional garnish is sauté potatoes, apple sauce and mustard. If cold, accompany the meat with an Olivier salad and horseradish sauce.

Paskha - Cheese Sweet
Kulich - Easter Bread

)

kuliches

kers yeast

epid water

cups milk

2 lb sugar

/2 tsp salt

/2 lb flour

egg yolks

la essence

sp nutmeg

b currants

lised fruit

d almonds

1 lb butter

eadcrumbs

Kulich is a sweet bread cooked in a
cylindrical mould. Failing this a large
empty canned vegetable tin can be used. As
it takes quite a bit of effort to make kulich
it is worth preparing at least two at a time as
a well-wrapped kulich keeps very well in the
fridge. It is delicious toasted for breakfast.

Dissolve the yeast in the water, warm the milk
slightly and add to it 1/4 k / 8 oz sugar, salt, the yeast
3/4 k /1 1/2 lb of flour. Beat hard and leave in a
very cool oven or a warm sheltered place for the
dough to rise. Beat the rest of the sugar with the egg
yolks until light and fluffy. Chop the crystalised fruit
and mix with the almonds and currants. Melt the butter.

When the dough has doubled in volume, gradually
blend in the butter, then the beaten eggs. Finally
add the flour. The dough should be very compact.
Knead well; the longer and harder it is kneaded
the better the kulich. Work the dried fruit
into the dough. Cover with a cloth and leave
to prove in a warm place for about 3 hours.

Grease the moulds with butter and dredge with breadcrumbs. Divide the dough between the moulds —they should be about 1/3 full— and leave to prove for another 30 minutes. Heat the oven to 150C / 300F and cook the kulich for 2 hours. It is cooked when a skewer comes out clean.

Remove from the oven and leave to cool in the tin for about 10 minutes and then remove from the mould. Roll lightly on the work top to keep the round shape.

Ice the top of the kulich with icing sugar dissolved in a teaspoon of milk or water and decorate with a red flower on top. Surround with coloured eggs which traditionally are served with the kulich.

Chokoladnaia Paskha
(Chocolate easter cheese)

Ingredients

1/2 k / 1 lb bitter chocolate

1 1/2 k curd cheese

6 egg yolks

2 cups sugar

2 cups cream

1 tsp vanilla extract

1/4 k / 8 oz butter

Place a large bowl over a pan of hot water and using an electric whisk beat together the egg yolks, the cream, sugar, butter and vanilla until light and fluffy. Continue beating with a wooden spoon until the mixture resembles a thin custard. Melt the chocolate and gradually mix into the egg mixture. Whip the egg whites and then gradually whip in the curd cheese until an even mixture is formed.

Pour the mixture into a 3 litre paskha mould previously lined with a muslim cloth. Tie the ends of the cloth together and put a weight on top.

Place the mould on a plate to catch the liquid which will be released and refrigerate. Remove from the mould before serving and decorate with raisins and place a flower on top.

Zavarnaia Paskha
(Sweet easter cheese)

Ingredients

4 1/2 lb / 2 k curd cheese

6 egg yolks

3/4 cup butter

1 1/2 cups sugar

1 cup ground almonds

1 cup currants

1/2 tsp almond extract

1 cup cream

The paskha mould is a four-sided wooden pyramid, open at the top and with a wooden base. Any carpenter should be able to make one, but failing that a new flower pot makes an excellent alternative.

Preparation for this paskha should begin 2 day in advance. Process the curd cheese until all lumps have been removed and it has become a creamy mass. Whisk the egg yolks with the butter and sugar for about 4 minutes at medium speed ending with another 2 minutes at maximum speed.

In another bowl whip the cream until it begins to thicken. Add the egg mixture together with the currants, almonds, almond extract and the cheese and mix well. Cook over a pan of hot water, or in a bain Marie, stirring continuously, until it begins to boil. Immediately remove from the heat and plunge the bowl into a larger one full of iced water. Continue stirring until the mass has cooled.

Pour the mixture into a 3 litre paskha mould previously lined with a muslim cloth. Tie the ends of the cloth together and put a weight on top. Place the mould on a plate to catch the liquid which will be released and refrigerate. Remove from the mould before serving and decorate with raisins and place a flower on top.

105

Ciraia Paskha
(Sweet easter cheese 2)

Ingredients

2 k / 4 1/2 lb curd cheese

1/2 k / 1 lb butter

1 tsp vanilla essence

150 g / 5 oz currants

1/2 k condensed milk, or 2 cups of
cream mixed with 1 1/2 cups sugar

150 g / 5 oz crystalised fruit

1 tsp grated lemon rind

2 hard boiled egg yolks

3 raw egg yolks

Melt the butter, vanilla and condensed milk in a bain Marie or bowl over hot water until it forms a mass and just comes to the boil. Remove from the heat and gradually incorporate the beaten egg yolks and the sieved cooked eggs. Stir well together. Chop the crystalised fruit and soak the currants in hot water.

Beat the cheese into the cream mixture with an electric whisk until smooth. Fold in the fruit and lemon rind. Pour into a cloth lined paskha mould (see previous recipe) and place on a plate to catch the liquid which will be released. Refrigerate with a weight on top for a couple of days.

Remove from the mould and decorate the top with a red carnation. Write the letters X.B in currants on each side and serve on a dish surrounded by coloured eggs.

 Soups from North and South

If we go back into the mists of time it is almost as if the Slavic race developed around the heat of the "pechca" (stove), eating soups with a "lochca" (wooden spoon) and black bread.

My personal theory is that Russian cuisine and Russian popular sculpture were born from these three simple bases, because even the crudest "lochca" has always been the object of love and care to its owner who marked it with his own personal signature by carving on the handle; and this custom gradually developed into real art.

Chinese lacquered art arrived in Russia along with the Mongol invasion, and this was later applied to the "lochca". Over the centuries the refinements on the handles of the "lochca" reached incredible lengths; lochca handles encrusted with enamel, silver and precious stones were used in the courts of the Tsars and in the houses of the rich merchants.

The "pechca" was, and in small villages still is, the heart and soul of the home; it was on this stove they cooked the bread and most of their meals. A pechca is usually made of clay or brick, with a metal oven door in the middle. In more wealthy households the stoves were faced with coloured tiles, and in the colder regions bunk beds were built at the sides and back of the stove so that the family could sleep in the warmth.

Every morning the housewife stoked up the fire with logs and put the bread in the oven. Later she would put salt pork and bones with cabbage and water into an earthenware pot, and with ingenious additions managed to cook a variety of dishes to vary the daily menus. These ingredients could include potatoes and root vegetables such as turnips, beetroot or carrots, and even dried mushrooms.

There was no hotplate on a peche so northern Russian cooking had no fried food, and their meals mainly consisted of soups, cereals, pastries and stews cooked in the oven. Of course not all peasants were poor, and after Ivan the Terrible overthrew the Mongol and Tartar tribes, the towns and villages began to

prosper. Trade with other regions brought new culinary ideas and ingredients, so that gradually the housewives learned to create and invent a delicious cuisine based on an ever-greater variety of soups.

Once again it is Anton Chekov who writes about a typically Russian dish:

"During Lent when people were still allowed to eat meat or drink milk, the houses smelled of borsch, but during the Greater Lent fast the smell was of fried sturgeon and sunflower oil...."

Talking of soup: I should think that Russian gastronomy has a greater variety of soups that any another other European country. There are soups made from fruit, from milk, meat and vegetables, sweet soups, sour soups, hot soups and cold ones. I can't give recipes for all of them, but I will give you my favourite ones from the ones I have tried out at least once. I will begin with the borsch mentioned by Chekov. It is perhaps the best known soup of all and has the most variations.

A perfect borsch, for example, is made from a salted smoked duck base. Many years ago shortly after my husband and I first opened our restaurant, the late Conde de los Andes —a famous Spanish gourmet and restaurant critic— came for dinner. We were chatting, and he mentioned that he had recently had a duck borsch at the house of some friends. I had never eaten, or even heard of duck borsch at that time. Years later when I was reading through an old Russian cookery book I found a recipe on how to salt and smoke duck and geese and how to use the bones, neck and wings to make a borsch.

I immediately went out to buy a large duck —it must have weighed almost seven pounds— and spent days trying to smoke the bird After using the meat in several dishes, I used the leftovers to make the stock for a soup. It really was worth all the effort.

Borsch from the north of Russia is perhaps the best known, but probably one of the best is from the Ukraine. Another good one is the Bielorussian Borsch, which is similar to the Ukrainian one but based on pork and sausage, while the Moldavian borsch is made from a chicken or fowl stock.

Borsch is probably the best known soup outside the Russian borders. But the greatest peasant soup which has been eaten in Russia throughout history,

through scarcity and adversity, through times of hunger, war and calamity, is the "mother of all Russian soups", cabbage soup or schti.

Nor must we forget the typical fish soups. Ukha is a soup made from tiny fresh water fish with the recipe varying from one region to another. The most famous Ukha is the one made on the lower reaches of the River Volga.

When I visited my father's hometown, Saratov, I tried unsuccessfully to find this soup. But probably the quantity of fish needed to make a good ukha is just not feasible today. Apparently this soup was prepared in three stages. The first stage was to prepare a good stock from dozens of fish too tiny to be eaten. That stock was boiled up again with more river fish to give it a good concentrated flavour, and finally fillets or steaks of sturgeon were poached in the broth. I have found a simpler more modest version which is, nonetheless, delicious.

Talking of fish soup, I am reminded of an amusing incident involving a bishop. My grandparents used to invite the local bishop to dine occasionally and their cook had to provide a meatless meal. Orthodox bishops, who are chosen by the church from among the monks, are not permitted to eat any meat. Apparently that day the cook was inspired and, naturally had indulged in a few drinks too many, and when he was summoned to the dining room to receive the congratulations from the bishop on his excellent fish soup he was delighted. "Of course it was delicious, your excellency," said a grinning Stephan the cook. "It was made from a good chicken stock ..." I have always followed Stephan's advice and use chicken stock as a base for my fish soups.

It is a shame that we in Europe cannot get the wide variety of fresh water fish which make these soups extra special. Russia, which is crossed by two major rivers, the Volga and the Don, has no such problems. This excerpt from Chekov's "The Steppe" tells it all:

"Egorushka looked into the bucket. It was full. He saw the ugly face of a young pike, and around it were wriggling crayfish and other small fish. The child put his hand into the bucket and stirred the water around; the pike disappeared beneath the crabs and a perch and a tench came to the surface. Vasia looked down into the bucket. His eyes filled with tears and the expression on his face softened as it had earlier when they had seen the fox. He took something from the water, put it in his mouth and began to chew.

"Boys!" screamed an astonished Stephan. "Vasia is eating a live mackerel. Ugh!"

"It isn't a mackerel. It's a gudgeon," replied Vasia, still chewing.

He took the fish tail from his mouth, looked at it happily, and returned to his mouth. As he chewed they could hear the crunching of fish bones, and to Egorushka it seemed as if the man before him was no longer human. Vasia's bulging cheeks, his dull eyes, his strange expression and the fish tail in his mouth as he chewed on the gudgeon, made him look more like an animal. Egorushka felt sad as he stood beside him. When he finished chewing, he walked pensively through the carts and made his way to the village."

In this section I have also included several recipes for cold soups, amongst which is a cold yogurt soup. It is like a Caucasian vichyssoise or gazpacho, refreshing and delicious with various possibilities. Use your imagination and you can easily make a yogurt soup to your own taste. You will be pleasantly surprised.

Borsch i Piroski
Beetroot Soup
and Piroski

Northern Borsch

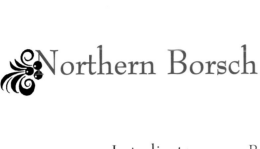

Ingredients

1/2 k / 1 lb breast of veal

300 g / 9 oz ham bones

2 beef bones

150 g / 5 oz bacon in one piece

1 cup shredded carrots

1 cup finely sliced onions

4 cups finely shredded cabbage

1/2 cup shredded turnips

3 unpeeled beetroot

1 cup diced potatoes

2 sticks celery

2 bay leaves

3 stalks parsley

Salt and pepper to taste

1 tbs vinegar

1 tsp sugar

2 cups sour cream

Put the meat, bones, bacon, salt, pepper, celery, parsley in a pressure cooker with 2 1/2 litres/ 4 pints water and cook for 20 minutes, or simmer in a casserole over a very low heat for 3 hours or until tender.

Place the unpeeled whole beetroots in another pan with sufficient water to cover, add a little salt and the vinegar. When they are cooked cool slightly reserving the cooking liquid. Peel and cut into julienne shreds.

Remove the meat from the broth and slice finely. Discard the bones and herbs. Return the meat to the broth and add all the vegetables, except the potatoes and beetroot. Cook over a medium heat for about 30 minutes. Add the potatoes and cook for another 15 minutes. Just before serving add the beetroot and its cooking liquid. Warm over a low heat without boiling, which would cause it to lose its lovely colour.

Serve with sour cream and piroski (recipe page 143). The soup is better made the previous day and reheated before serving.

Ukrainian Borsch

Ingredients

75 g /3 oz lard

600 g / 1 1/2 lb beetroot

800 g/ 1 3/4 lb cabbage

500 g / 1 lb potatoes

200 g/ 7 oz carrots

200 g / 7 oz turnips

1 large onion

2 whole cloves garlic

2 tsp crushed garlic

1 tsp sugar

1 tbs vinegar

2 bay leaves

1/4 k / 8 oz stewing beef

1/4 k / 8 oz pork

A few ham and beef bones

1 cup cooked white beans

2 tbs tomato paste

Salt and pepper

Cut the beetroot, carrots, turnips and onion into julienne shreds and soften them in the lard and then stir in the sugar, vinegar, salt and pepper and tomato paste. Remove from the heat.

In a pressure cooker put 3 litres of water and the meat, bones, bay leaves and garlic and cook for 20 minutes. Open the cooker and remove the meat and bones. Or cook in a covered casserole over a very low heat for about 3 hours until tender. Cool and remove the grease from the top of the broth. Shred the meat and return to the broth with the cooked vegetables, the sliced cabbage, the diced potatoes and chopped parsley. Bring back to the boil and simmer for about 30 minutes. Add the beans and leave to rest for a few hours.

Reheat over a low heat. Serve in a tureen with sour cream served separately and warm piroski (recipe page 143) wrapped in a napkin.

Schti
(Cabbage soup)

Ingredients

1/4 k / 8 oz pickled cabbage

1 small or half medium cabbage

1 onion

1 carrot

8 cups beef stock

2 tomatoes

2 potatoes

1 bay leaf

2 tbs pork lard

Salt and pepper to taste

2 cups sour cream

(This soup can also be made without
pickled cabbage and tomato)

Rinse the pickled cabbage and finely shred the fresh cabbage and onion. Slice the carrots into rounds. Sauté all the vegetables in lard and when they begin to soften pour over the stock and cook over a medium heat for about 30 minutes. Add the diced potatoes, tomatoes and bay leaves and cook for another 15 minutes. Remove the bay leaf and adjust the seasoning. Serve with sour cream separately.

Sup iz Krasnovo Lobio
(Georgian red bean and walnut soup)

Ingredients

200 g / 7 oz red beans

50 g /2 oz peeled walnuts

2 cloves garlic

2 tbs chopped parsley

1 tbs dill weed

1 onion

1 tbs vinegar

Salt and pepper

Soak the beans overnight before cooking them with the onion and garlic in 1 1/2 litres/3 pints, of salted water. When soft blend or pass through a mouli, add the vinegar. Crush the walnuts with the parsley and dill and sprinkle over the soup and adjust seasoning.

Rakovoi Sup
(Cold freshwater crayfish soup)

Ingredients

1 1/2 k /3 lb freshwater
crayfish

1 glass dry sherry

1 tbs corn flour

1 tsp dill weed

1/2 k / 1 lb chopped tomatoes
(fresh or tinned) a little milk to
dilute corn flour

2 bay leaves

Parsley

2 shallots

Salt and pepper to taste

1/4 litre sour cream

Prepare a court bouillon by combining 1 1/2 litres / 2 1/2 pints of water with the bay leaf, parsley, salt and pepper, shallots and sherry. Bring to the boil and simmer for about 15 minutes. Add the crayfish and simmer for a further 10 minutes. Cool and peel the crayfish.

Blend the heads and shells of the crayfish adding a little of the court bouillon. Press through a sieve with the remainder of the court bouillon, adding the strained tomato, the corn flour diluted with the milk and the dill. Blend the crayfish meat and add to the soup. Return to the heat and stir with a wooden spoon until it begins to thicken. Remove from the heat and add the cream. Check the seasoning and add more if necessary.

Refrigerate for at least 6 hours and serve in consommé cups sprinkled with chopped dillweed.

Rassolnik
(Chicken soup with pickled cucumbers)

Ingredients

2 k / 4 1/2 lb chicken necks,
wings and giblets

1 veal kidney

3 carrots

1 cup chopped spinach

2 sticks celery

1 tbs chopped parsley and thyme

2 bay leaves

1 cup chopped pickled cucumber

1 cup of pickling liquid

7 pints 2 1/2 litres water

1 cup diced potatoes

4 tbs sour cream

Salt and pepper to taste

Dash of vinegar to cook the kidney

Make the stock with the chicken giblets and pieces, vegetables and herbs. Meanwhile clean the kidney and wash in several changes of cold water. Cook in salted water with the vinegar for 15 minutes.

Strain the stock, cool and remove the fat from the surface. Skin the chicken giblets and pieces and shred the meat, dicing the giblets. Return to the stock and add the pickles and their juice. Cut the kidney through the middle and remove the gristle and nerves. Slice into thin slices and add to the stock with the potatoes. Cook the soup for another 15 minutes. Just before serving stir in the sour cream. This soup is also delicious served cold.

Botvinia
(Freshwater fish soup)

Ingredients

1 k / 2 1/4 lb spinach

1/4 k / 8 oz sorrel

6 cups kvas or 3 cups beer and 3
cups water

2 cups salted water

6 slices freshwater fish

(e.g. salmon, trout or carp)

12 tails freshwater crayfish

2 chopped gerkins

Salt and pepper to taste

1 bay leaf

Clean and cook the green vegetables in a little salted water. Process them or pass through a mouli grinder, leaving slightly runny. Cook the crayfish in 2 cups of water seasoned with salt, pepper and the bay leaf. Remove after about 8 minutes, and in the same water lightly cook the slices of fish. Remove from the broth and keep to one side covered with a clean cloth.

Peel the crayfish and add to the fish. Add the cooking water to the vegetable purée along with the kvas or the diluted beer and bring to the boil. This soup is usually served in a soup tureen with the fish, decorated with the crayfish and gerkins, on a separate platter. Each diner serves himself to the fish and adds his own soup.

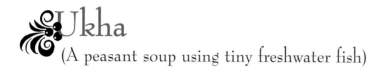Ukha
(A peasant soup using tiny freshwater fish)

Ingredients

1 k / 2 1/4 lb small freshwater fish

6 fillets of trout

1 large turnip

1 large onion

2 carrots

1 stick celery

1 egg white

1 bay leaf

Salt and pepper

1 tsp dill weed

6 rounds fried bread

Cook the small fish in 2 litres of water with the remaining ingredients except the egg white, trout and dill. Sieve and clarify with the lightly beaten egg whites. About 10 minutes before serving poach the trout fillets in the stock and sprinkle the chopped dillweed on the top. Serve with a garnish of fried bread.

Sup c Gribami y c Lapchoy
(Bielorussian mushroom soup with pasta)

Ingredients

1 k / 2 1/4 lb beef bones

1/2 k / 1 lb stewing beef

100 g / 4 oz dried mushrooms
(soaked overnight)

2 large onions

2 tbs flour

2 bay leaves

Dash of vinegar

Salt and pepper to taste

4 tbs vegetable oil

Pasta

1/4 k / 8 oz flour

1 egg

1 tsp oil

1 egg shell of water

1/4 tsp salt

Crushed peppercorns

Cook the meat, the bones, mushrooms with their strained liquid, salt, pepper and bay leaf in a pressure cooker for about 20 minutes, or for about 3 hours in a covered casserole over a very low heat. Chill, discard the bones and bay leaf. Cut the meat and the mushrooms into thin strips. Degrease the stock and return the meat and vegetables to it.

Slice the onion into thin strips and fry over a low heat until golden brown, add the flour and continue cooking and stirring until it darkens slightly, pour on the dash of vinegar. Then add to the broth and bring to the boil before serving.

Pasta

Mix and knead all the ingredients for the pasta. Cover with a cloth and leave to rest in the fridge for about an hour. Roll out as finely as possible and cut into very thin strips or use a pasta roller, and then cut these into 3 or 4 cm / 1 1/2 inch lengths. Add these to the hot soup and cook for about 5 minutes.

Sup iz Prastakvachi
Iced Yogurt Soup

Sup iz Prastakvachi
(Iced yogurt soup)

Ingredients

4 yogurts

2 yogurt cartons of single cream

2 finely chopped hard-boiled eggs

1 coffee cup soaked currants

2 peeled and finely chopped cucumbers

2 finely chopped spring onions

Salt and pepper to taste

1 tsp dill weed

4 yogurt cartons iced water

Mix all the ingredients together in a glass or china bowl. Add a little extra water if it seems too thick. Refrigerate for several hours. Serve the tureen buried in a bowl of crushed ice.

Gribnoi Sup
(Mushroom soup)

Ingredients

12 large mushrooms

1 sliced carrot

1 chopped onion

1 cup diced potato

1 tbs corn flour

1 bay leaf

1 tsp chopped parsley

Salt and pepper to taste

8 cups chicken stock

1 tbs dill weed

2 tbs vegetable oil

Clean and cut the mushrooms into thin slices. Fry the mushroom and onions in a little oil. Add the stock, carrot, bay leaf, salt and pepper. Cover and cook for 15 minutes, add the potatoes and continue cooking for a further 10 minutes.

Dilute the corn flour with a little water and add to the soup, stirring all the time. Serve the soup with the chopped dill sprinkled on top.

Sviokolnik
(Cold beetroot soup)

Ingredients

4 beetroot

4 cups clarified beef stock

3 cups kvas or 1 1/2 cups beer
and 1 1/2 cups water

1 cup finely chopped cucumber

2 hard-boiled eggs chopped

Salt, pepper and dill weed to taste

Dash of vinegar

2 cups sour cream

Cook the whole unpeeled beetroot with salt and dash of vinegar. Keep about 3 cups of the cooking water. Peel the beetroot and cut into fine shreds. Mix all the ingredients, except the sour cream. Serve very cold with the sour cream separately.

Ocrochka
(Cold beef soup)

Ingredients

1/2 cup cooked beef cut into
1/2 cm dice
1/2 cup diced boiled ham
1/2 cup shredded tongue
(recipe page 70)
2 chopped hard-boiled eggs
1/2 cup chopped spring onion,
dill and parsley
3 cups chicken stock
3 cups kvas or 2 cups beer
and 1 cup water
Sour cream to serve separately

Mix all the ingredients together in a soup tureen and refrigerate for several hours. Sink the tureen in a bowl of crushed ice and serve with the cream separately.

Vegetables Eggs and Pasta

With the exception of the south of Russia, where they abound, green vegetables are usually served as a garnish for meat or fish, or in salad, rather than as a separate course. This is probably because the only vegetables available on the market during the long winter months are potatoes, root vegetables such as carrots and turnips and the ubiquitous red and green cabbage. Thus greens are only eaten during the short spring and even shorter summers.

I have also included a few typical Lenten dishes which use potatoes and green vegetables. As in other European countries Russians cook eggs in many ways: as omelettes, fried, scrambled and particularly hard boiled stuffed eggs, either hot or cold. There are many kinds of pastas, pasties and pies; pasta is combined with meat, soups, or milk in sweet and savoury dishes. Pirogui or pasties are so important in Russian cooking that they merit a chapter of their own.

Buckwheat kasha is the most typical grain of the north of Russia. They use it in the same way as we use rice; it is also added to wheat flour to make black bread, nowadays we can buy it in the rest of Europe in specialised food shops. The most common use for buckwheat is as a garnish for meat or spiced up with onions, mushrooms, walnuts etc. as a first course. They also use it cooked with milk and sweetened with honey. My recipe is delicious served either alone or as an accompaniment for other dishes.

Pelmeni are dishes which originated in the Russian Asiatic lands and became incorporated into Russian cooking over the centuries. There are Siberian pelmeni, for which I have included a recipe, but there are dozens of other variations on the same theme. In Uzbekistan they make a similar dish called "manty", which are like pelmeni stuffed with minced lamb and shaped into little money bags. They are usually eaten with yogurt and chopped mint. Chebureki is the version which has come to us from central Asia. In this case the pastry is stuffed with finely chopped fried onion, rice, chunks of lamb, and fried in oil. They also make something similar in Ukraine but with the stuffing made from fried onion and pickled cabbage.

Siberian Pelmeni
(Siberian meat pasties)

Ingredients

Stuffing:

1/2 k / 1 lb minced veal

1/4 k / 8 oz minced pork

1 large onion

1 tsp chopped parsley

1 tsp chopped dill weed

1 tsp salt

1/2 tsp ground pepper

Pastry:

2 cups flour

1 egg

1/2 cup water

1/2 tsp salt

1 tbs vegetable oil

Make pastry by kneading all pastry ingredients for 5 mins on a pastry slab. Cover with a damp cloth and leave to rest. Chop or mince the onion as finely as possible and mix together with the remaining stuffing ingredients.

Roll out the pastry until very thin. Cut into rounds with a pastry cutter or a water glass. Place a teaspoonful of the stuffing on each pastry disc, damp the edges with cold water. Fold each disc in half and seal well with the prongs of a fork, then join the two ends together by gluing them with a moistened finger tip.

Bring a pan of water to the boil and add a good pinch of salt. Gently lower pelmeni into the boiling water a dozen at a time. Simmer for 5 minutes and remove with a slotted spoon. Keep warm while cooking the rest of the pelmeni. Serve with melted butter or sour cream.

To serve as a garnish with soup, simply add the pasties directly to the broth and simmer for about 5-8 minutes. Another way of serving pelmeni is to put the poached pasties into an oven-proof dish, cover with sour cream and sprinkle with grated cheese and brown under the grill.

1

2

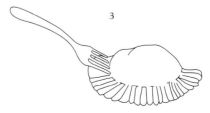

3

Grechnevaia Kasha
(Buckwheat kasha)

Ingredients

1/2 k / 1 lb buckwheat

2 tbs butter

1/2 tsp salt

2 medium onions

1/2 k / 1 lb mushrooms or boletus

2 tbs vegetable oil

Melt the butter in a heavy oven-proof pan and in it lightly brown the buckwheat grains, salt and add sufficient water to cover. Cover and cook in a low oven for about 30 minutes. Turn off the oven and leave the pan in the oven a further hour to cool completely.

Fry the finely chopped onions in the oil until golden. Add the sliced mushrooms and cook a few minutes more. Just before serving add the onions and mushrooms to the cooked kasha.

Kurnik
(Chicken pie)

Ingredients

1/2 k / 1 lb ready-made
flaky pastry

1 cold chicken poached in stock

2 tbs butter

3 cups cooked rice

5 hard-boiled eggs

1 cups sliced cooked mushrooms

Salt, pepper and dill weed

1 raw egg lightly beaten

Sauce

Reduced chicken stock

2 tbs flour

2 tbs cream

Juice half lemon

Remove chicken from the carcass and cut into bite-sized pieces. Chop the eggs and melt the butter. In a large bowl mix the chicken, rice, eggs, mushrooms, salt and pepper, dillweed and butter.

Divide flaky pastry into two halves. Roll out one half into a circle about 14 inches in diameter and place the filling in the centre. Roll out the second half and place it over the filling, sealing the edges with a little water. Glaze with the beaten egg. Cut a hole about 1/2 inch in the centre to allow the steam to escape. If you like you can cut a piece of pastry into the shape of a chicken to decorate the pie. Cook in a pre-heated 250C / 500 F oven for about 20 minutes.

Sauce:

Reduce the chicken stock. Add the flour and stir well over the heat until the sauce has thickened. Add the cream and lemon juice just before serving.

Serve the pie whole and cut into individual portions, with the sauce handed round separately.

Iatzi c Gribami
Mushrooms and Eggs

Wild mushroom stuffing

Ingredients

1 k /2 1/4 lb oyster or other
wild mushroom
1 large chopped onion
4 tbs butter
1 cup cooked bulgar or buckwheat
Salt and pepper to taste

Clean the mushrooms by wiping carefully with a cloth. Do not wash them unless they are very dirty, in which case rinse very quickly and immediately dry on kitchen paper. Slice into thin strips.

Cook the onion in the butter until golden, add the mushrooms and parsley, stirring as you go. Add salt and pepper with the cooked buckwheat (recipe page 132). Chill and use to fill pirogui.

Kuliebiaka
Salmon pie

Kuliebiaka
(Salmon pie)

Ingredients

1/2 k / 1 lb ready-made puff
pastry
3/4 k lightly steamed salmon
1 cup cooked rice
1/2 cup slices cooked mushrooms
1/2 cup sliced and softened onions
1/2 cup white sauce
3 hard-boiled eggs
1 cup soaked Chinese rice noodles
1/4 tsp salt and pinch ground pepper
1/4 tsp dill

In my opinion this salmon pasty is one of the best inventions of Russian cuisine. To make a genuine kuliebiaka you should use 'vesiga', a form of gelatine made from the spinal cord of the sturgeon. As this is not generally available I substitute Chinese rice noodles which have a similar texture.

Roll out half the pastry into a rectangle to fit an oven tray. Mix all the filling ingredients together and pile up on the pastry. Roll out the other half of the pastry and cover the filling-Seal well lightly pressing down on the two layers of pastry.

Beat the egg yolk with a teaspoon of water and using a pastry brush glaze the crust. If there is a little pastry left over you can decorate by cutting into leaf shapes and arranging attractively on top.

Cook in a preheated hot oven for about 40 minutes. Serve hot with a cup of fish or chicken broth on the side.

# Meat stuffing

Ingredients

1 k /2 1/4 lb stewing beef

1 k / 2 1/4 lb cow's foot

1 large onion

1 carrot

1 stick celery

1 leek

1 turnip

1 tsp salt

1/4 tsp ground black pepper

Put all the ingredients in a pressure cooker, add sufficient water to cover and cook for about 40 minutes (the time depends on the pressure of the cooker and the toughness of the meat) Or cook in a covered casserole for about 3 1/2 hours over a very low heat or until tender. Put to one side until cool. Remove the bones and chop the rest as finely as possible.

To this filling you can add 1 cup of cooked rice or 2 cups cooked buckwheat (recipe page 132).

Fish

My father was born in Saratov, a city on the banks of the great Volga River, the "Mother of Russia". He used to tell me stories of his youth and of his escapades with the sons of the fishermen with whom he went to fish, swim or generally get up to mischief. Many times he went to the homes of his friends and ate the famous ukha, fishermen's soup, and other stews made from the river fauna. Whether it was the truth or simply nostalgia, he swore that nowhere else in the world could one eat a better fish soup.

Russia is a land of many lakes and legendary rivers: the Volga, the Don and the Dnieper. The majority of our fish dishes are made from freshwater fish from these rivers and lakes. Unfortunately it isn't easy to find many varieties of freshwater fish in our western European markets, and for this reason some of my recipes have been adapted to use other more easily available fish. Although I have not included any recipe using eel, I was amused by the Chekov story "The Tale of the eel" which depicts so accurately the customs, lives and aspirations of the ordinary Russian people. Here are a few paragraphs…

"Mind you don't cut your fingers," warned the master, hearing the axe under the water. "Efimzzz, go away! I will catch the eel. You're useless."

He split the log, lifted it out of the water a short way and managed to get his fingers into the gills of the eel.

"I've got it! Boys, don't push…keep still…there it's out!" Eventually the large head of the eel came to the surface, and behind it a shiny black body at least a metre long. The eel struggled and tried to escape.

Triumphant smiles lit up all their faces, and after a few minutes of silent admiration they began to shout: "We got it, we got it!"

"It's a fantastic eel!" Efim stammered, scratching its belly. "It must weigh at least 10 pounds."

"At least," agreed the Master. "And look how fat it is. It's almost ready to burst out of its skin. Ooh! Aah!"

But suddenly the eel wriggled its tail so violently that it escaped and the fishermen looked on as it dived back into the river. They plunged their hands in after it, but it was too late. The eel had gone for ever......."

Sturgeon is usually made into kebabs, a delicious recipe which comes from the Caucasus in the south. The secret of a juicy kebab is to cut the fish into fairly large chunks and leave them to marinate for a couple of hours before cooking.

In some parts of the Caucasus they use yogurt to marinate the fish; in other regions, where the population is predominantly Moslem, instead of bacon they use lamb suet; another variation is to sprinkle the kebab with grenadine syrup.

Sturgeon is mentioned again in M.A. Sholojov in his "Peaceful River Don":

"His father and Grishka managed to pull the trammel net from the junk room into the hall.

"Bring me some twine and a large needle, quickly!" Grigori shouted to Duniasha. They lit the light in the kitchen and Daria began to mend the net. The old woman cradled the baby and grumbled:

"You're always trying to invent something new, old man. You would be better off going to bed, paraffin is more expensive every day, and it doesn't seem to matter to you if you waste it. You won't catch any fish now. Where will this lead us? You could drown us all. Look at the weather. Look, look at that lightening! Lord Jesus Christ, Queen of the Heavens...."

Suddenly the kitchen was lit up with a blinding blue light and they all fell silent. They could hear the rain beating on the wooden slats over the window. Suddenly there was a deafening roll of thunder. Duniasha let out a scream and hid her head in the net. Daria made the sign of the cross over the doors and windows.

The old woman looked with frightened eyes at the cat which had hidden beneath her feet.

"Duniasha! Get it out... Queen of the Heavens, forgive this sinner. Duniasha, put this cat out into the garden. Go away, spirit of the devil."

Shaking with laughter Grigori dropped the net on the ground.

"What's the matter with you all? Shut up!" shouted Pantelei Prokofievich. "Hurry up and finish that net. I told you not to forget it."

"You won't catch anything now," said the old woman trying to dissuade them from going out.

"You don't understand, so shut up. Now is the best time to catch sturgeon on the sand bank. They are frightened by the storm and swim close to the bank. The water comes rushing down. You, Duniasha, go out and see if the current is running."

Unwillingly Duniasha went towards the door.

"Who will get into the water? You can't do it Daria, you could catch a cold on your chest," insisted the old woman.

"Grishka and I will go. We will call on Axinia and some of the women to bring another net."

"Have we got the sacks? I know we will come back with a good sized fish."

They went outside. The rain, which was pouring down on to the damp earth, formed foam on the puddles and streamed down into the Don. Grigori went ahead and a strange happiness filled his mind.

"Take care, father, there is a ditch here."

"How dark it is!"

"Don't leave me, Axiushka, we'll go to jail together," said Malasha, letting out a loud guffaw.

"Look, Grigori, isn't that the Maidannikov's boat?"

"Yes it is."

"Here....we can begin here," shouted Pantelei Prokofievich, trying to make himself heard over the noise of the wind.

"We can't hear a thing, grandfather" Malasha shouted in a hoarse voice.

"Get in, God help us....I'll go on in first...... I said I would go in first....Are you deaf, Malasha? Don't pull like that. I said I'd go in first.....Grigori, Grishka! Let Asinia go along the bank!"

There was a loud roaring over the Don, the rain was falling like a horizontal curtain of water. Carefully feeling the way with his feet, Grigori got into the river and the water came up to his waist. The icy cold wrapped itself like a band around his heart. The waves broke against his face, forcing him to close his eyes. The fishing net filled like a balloon, pulling him under. The stick attached to the net was pulled from his hands... Deeper and deeper. A step. His feet slipped. The current pulled him violently, and sucked him under. The blackness of the deep frightened him as he had never feared before. He kicked out against the soft ground. A fish knocked against his knee.

"Go on, go on!," he heard his father shouting from the distant darkness. The net moved again and pulled him to the bottom. Grigori lost his step again and was forced to swim as he spat the water from his mouth.

"Are you still alive, Axinia?"

"For the time being, yes."

"Has it stopped raining?"

"It's beginning to rain again."

"Don't shout. If my father hears you he will be angry with us."

"Don't be afraid of father."

They pulled the net in silence. The water was like a sticky mass which made movement difficult.

"Grishka, there are some roots on the bank, we will have to go round them."

A dreadful tug pulled Grigori into the river. There was a loud splash as if a huge rock had fallen into the pool...."

There is also a Russian-Jewish culinary tradition, today almost forgotten, which developed alongside the Russian one over many generations.

Borscht, for example, is in this tradition because no pork meat is used when making it. Of all the Russian-Jewish dishes, the most famous is stuffed carp. As with so many other freshwater fish it is difficult to find this fish today. I have substituted sea bass and it makes a delicious alternative.

It is also almost impossible to find sudak (pike) today in our lakes. Its firm white flesh is similar to hake and it too makes a good alternative. I make pike or hake Novgorod style, after that important city built by the Scandinavians on the banks of the River Voljov as it flows into Lake Ilmes. It is a delicious "papillote" recipe.

Shashlik iz Ositrini
(Sturgeon or sword-fish kebab)

Ingredients

1 1/2 k / 3 1/2 lbs sword-fish
chopped into 4 cm dice

3 green peppers cut in 3 cm squares

3 or 4 small onions in medium slices

6 slices bacon

6 cherry tomatoes

4 cloves garlic (sliced)

3 tbs olive oil

Juice 1 lemon

1 tsp salt

1/4 tsp pepper

3 lemons to garnish

Mix the lemon juice with the oil, garlic, salt and pepper. Pour over the diced sword-fish, mix together and leave to marinate for a couple of hours. Thread the chunks of fish on to 6 kebabs with the bacon, pepper, onion and tomato, ending with the tomato. The bacon should go alongside the fish so that its fat keeps the flesh moist. Grill over the barbecue turning several times until cooked. Serve with rice and salad.

Ositrina po Ruski
Russian Style Salmon

Ositrina ili Lososina po Ruski
(Russian style sturgeon or salmon)

Ingredients

2 k / 4 1/2 lb salmon or
sturgeon (tail end if possible)

1 bouquet garni

2 lemons

1 glass white wine

1 sliced onion

1 sliced carrot

Salt and pepper to taste

Garnish

1 litre mayonnaise

6 tomatoes

A few lettuce leaves

2 small cucumbers

2 leaves gelatine dissolved in a
little hot water

4 tbs chopped capers

Half fill a fish kettle with water. Add the bouquet garni, white wine, salt and a few peppercorns. Bring to the boil and simmer about 20 minutes. Cool slightly and place the fish in the court bouillon. When it comes back to the boil, reduce the heat and simmer for about 10 minutes. Leave the fish in the water until cold. Remove from the liquid and skin the fish. Place on a bed of lettuce on a large platter. Cover with mayonnaise and decorate with thin slices of unskinned cucumber to resemble fish scales. With a pastry brush spread a thin coat of gelatine over the cucumber slices.

Cut the top off each tomato and empty out the flesh. Mix the capers with the mayonnaise and fill each tomato with the mixture. Place the tomatoes and sliced lemons around the fish. Serve a Salad Olivier separately.

Forel c Sous iz Orej
Trout with walnut sauce

Forel c Sous iz Orej
(Trout with walnut sauce)

Ingredients

6 whole trout
1 bouquet garni
1 lemon
Salt and pepper to taste

Sauce

1/4 k / 8 oz peeled and chopped walnuts
3 tbs butter
4 tbs chopped onions
1 tsp chopped garlic
2 tbs flour
2 cups broth from cooking fish
2 tsp white wine vinegar
1/2 tsp crushed saffron
1/4 tsp ground cinnamon and
cloves (less cloves than cinnamon)
Salt and pepper to taste

Make a court bouillon and leave to cool. Put the fish in the court bouillon and bring to the boil. Reduce the heat and simmer for about 6 minutes. Remove the fish and reserve 2 cups of the broth.

To make the sauce: Fry onion and garlic in the butter until golden. Add flour and stir until it begins to take colour and pour in the broth. Bring to boil and simmer until the sauce has thickened slightly. Add remaining ingredients, season and pour the sauce over the trout. Serve with a garnish of boiled potatoes.

Forel po Ruski
(Russian trout)

Ingredients

6 whole trout

1 cup thinly sliced mushrooms

1/2 cup white sauce

3 cups sour cream

2 tbs Worcester sauce

4 tbs butter

2 tbs vegetable oil

Flour

Clean the trout and dry on kitchen paper. Dredge with flour and a little salt. Heat butter and oil in a frying pan and fry trout until golden. Discard the fat. Mix the remaining ingredients together and pour over the trout in the frying pan. Reduce over a low flame for 6 to 10 minutes until the trout are cooked. Serve with boiled rice or steamed potatoes.

Stuchka po Yieovski
(Stuffed carp, pike, or sea bass)

Ingredients

1 k / 2 1/4 lb sea bass

(or carp)

6 slices white bread

1 cup single cream

3 egg yolks

1 tsp chopped parsley

1/2 tbs sugar

1/4 tsp white pepper

1 tsp salt

Sauce

2 tbs grated horseradish

2 cups sour cream

Court bouillon

1 glass white wine

1 bouquet garni and the fish head

1 carrot

1 onion

Clean and dry the fish and reserve the fish head for the stock. With the back of a knife scale the fish and remove the flesh leaving 3/4 inch attached to the skin.

Make court bouillon using all the ingredients. Bring to the boil and leave to simmer for about 20 mins. Leave to cool.

Soak the bread in the cream and mix in egg yolks, parsley, sugar, salt and pepper and the finely chopped fish flesh. Stir well and stuff the mixture into the fish skin. Sew the fish with fine thread and wrap in a muslin cloth. Tie well so it remains intact during the cooking. Place in the court bouillon and bring to the boil. Simmer about 10 minutes. Leave to cool in the liquid. Remove the cloth and the thread. Serve on a platter decorated with boiled potatoes. Mix the grated horseradish with the sour cream and serve separately.

Sudak po Novgorodski
(Novgorod pike)

Ingredients

6 thick slices pike or hake

6 cups sour cream

2 tsp dill weed

Salt and pepper

Mix sour cream with 1/2 tsp salt and 1/4 tsp pepper and dill weed. Place the fish slices in individual oven-proof dishes, or in a single layer in one large dish. Cover with the sour cream mixture and seal with foil. Place in a preheated moderate oven and cook for 20 minutes, or until cooked. Serve with plain boiled potatoes.

Ribnie Kotletki c Gribnom Sousom
(Fish balls with mushroom sauce)

Ingredients

1.2 k. fillets of hake or other
white fish

1 1/2 cups white breadcrumbs

1 beaten egg

1 tsp salt

1/4 tsp ground pepper

1 tsp dill weed

1 cup butter

1 cup toasted breadcrumbs

1/2 cup vegetable oil to fry

Mushroom sauce

1 small finely chopped onion

1 1/2 tbs butter

2 cups finely sliced mushroom

1 tsp flour

1/2 tsp salt

1/2 cup milk

1 cup sour cream

Skin and bone the raw fish and mince or chop finely. Soak the white breadcrumbs in a little milk and then squeeze out the surplus liquid. Mix the fish with the breadcrumbs, add egg, salt, pepper and dill weed.

Make 12 balls out of the fish mixture and another 12 balls out of softened butter. Insert a butter ball into the centre of each fish ball and seal the hole. Roll fish balls in the toasted breadcrumbs, pressing in well. Leave to rest for about 30 mins. Heat the oil in a pan and fry the fish balls, turning when each side is cooked. Drain on kitchen paper.

Sauce

Melt the butter in a small pan and fry the onions until half cooked. Add the sliced mushrooms and continue frying stirring all the time. Add the flour and cook until golden. Season with salt and pepper and gradually add the milk and continue stirring until thickened. Remove from the heat and add the sour cream.

Serve the fish balls with boiled potatoes and with the sauce in a separate dish.

Poultry and Game

The names of most of the great masters of Russian cuisine have sunk almost without trace. Their inventions were not immortalised with the identity of their inventors, but rather with the names of their employers or honoured guests. We have been left with only two exceptions: the great chef Olivier, already mentioned for his Russian salad, and Pozarskii, the owner and chef of an inn in the small town of Torzhok, a regular stop to change the horses on the road between Moscow and St. Petersburg.

Pozarskii made chicken croquettes second to none. He used partridge or pheasant mixed with minced chicken or veal, gently fried them in fresh butter until golden, before garnishing with wild mushrooms in a sour cream sauce. His fame spread across the whole of northern Russia, until eventually he was immortalised with four verses dedicated to him by the great Russian poet

Pushkin. I believe that the recipe I have found could possibly be his original one.

One cannot talk about poultry in the Russian kitchen without mentioning goose and swan. Goose is a wonderful bird which, except for the French who use it for foie gras, has virtually disappeared from our tables – although it is creeping back into favour once more. Until turkey arrived in Europe, including Russia, from America, goose was the favourite bird at Christmas time. In old cookery books I came across dozens of recipes for preparing and cooking goose. In my opinion, goose is one of the most delicious of all poultry. But for the bird to be tender it must be young and well fed, if not it can be tough and fatty. If you can get hold of a good free range goose, I thoroughly recommend one for next Christmas.

Another bird which now has almost completely disappeared from the Russian table is the swan, and at one time swans' eggs were even considered a great delicacy. In old Russia, and even until the beginning of the 19th Century it was traditional to serve this majestic bird, reconstructed in all its beauty, roasted for wedding banquets. There is a wonderful painting by Konstantin Makovski of the wedding banquet in which a servant is carrying a magnificent

swan on a huge silver platter. In our "El Cosaco" restaurant in the old part of Madrid we took this painting as the inspiration for a mural.

I have also included several original recipes for chicken. For example, a chicken "tabaka" uses a really small poussin – the smaller the better. But you need a good eye and a lot of patience to get the fat to exactly the right temperature so that it browns well and cooks through without burning. Although it is worth all the effort, it is not a recipe I would really recommend to a beginner cook.

There is also a recipe for that classic dish, Chicken Kiev. Kiev is the capital of the Ukraine; it was the first capital city of the Russian state and has been called the "Mother of Russian Cities". It stands on the estuaries of the Rivers Dniéper and Desná. Chicken Kiev is one of its great treasures, along with its ancient monasteries and wonderful church music which makes it one of Russia's great musical centres.

Gus c Iablokami
Goose with apples

&Gus c Iablokami
(Goose with apples)

Ingredients

3-4 k / 6-7 lb goose
2 large cooking apples
2 cups / 500g / 1 lb diced stale bread
1 tbs chopped parsley
1 tbs chopped dill weed
2 tbs chopped celery
1/2 cup / 125g / 4 oz pinenuts or
cooked sliced chestnuts
1 finely chopped onion
2 tbs / 30g / 1 oz butter

Stock

2 carrots
1 stick celery
Salt and pepper
Giblets from the bird

Garnish

1 jar red currant or cranberry
jam or sauce
6 small apples

Clean the bird well and salt inside and out. Leave to stand while preparing other ingredients.

Make stock with the giblets, 3/4 litre/26 fl oz water and remaining ingredients. Cook until well flavoured. Leave to go cold and then remove the fat from the surface.

Fry onions in the butter until golden. Chop apples into small chunks and add to the onions. Add remaining ingredients and stuff both ends of the bird. Preheat oven to 200C/400F/Gas 6. Roast the goose for 45 minutes per kilo/ 20 minute per lb or until cooked basting with the stock as it cooks. Remove the goose to a dish and keep warm. Skim fat from the top of the juice which remains.

Garnish

Core the small apples and fill the centre with the currant jam. Roast 30 mins in a moderate oven. These can be prepared before cooking the goose and returned to the oven to heat shortly before serving.

Serve the goose whole surrounded by the baked apples on a large platter with the gravy in a sauce boat.

Utka c Vichinimi
Duck with cherries

Utka c Vichinimi
(Duck with cherries)

Ingredients

6 duck legs (1st and 2nd joints)

giblets from 2 ducks

1 glass brandy

2 large onions

4 carrots

2 bay leaves

Salt and pepper to taste

Juice 1 lemon

500g / 1 lb tin cherries with juice
(unsweetened)

2 tsp corn flour

2 cups / 450 ml / 16 fl oz stock
made from duck giblets

Bring to the boil the duck giblets with 1 tsp salt, pepper, bay leaves and 1 onion in 3/4 litre/26 fl oz water and simmer for about 45 minutes.

Clean the duck legs and rub in salt and pepper and arrange in a single layer in an oven proof dish. Arrange slices of the peeled carrots and the onions around the duck.

Place in a pre-heated 200C/400F/Gas 6 oven. After about 45 mins skim the fat from the dish and flame with the brandy. Reduce the temperature to 180C/350F and return duck legs to the oven . Baste occasionally with the stock until the legs are well cooked. The time will depend on the size of the legs, but it should take about 1 1/2 to 2 hours.

Remove the duck from the dish and blend the carrots and onions in a food processor before sieving. Dissolve the corn flour in the cherry juice and lemon juice. Add to this the sieved duck sauce and bring to the boil, stirring all the time until thickened.

Serve the duck legs surrounded by the cherries. The sauce should be served separately.

173

Kievskie Kotlety
Chicken Kiev

Kievskie Kotlety
(Chicken Kiev)

Ingredients

6 skinned chicken breasts
with the wing bone remaining

6-2 cm / 1 inch dice of very cold
butter mixed with finely chopped parsley

Salt and pepper

2 beaten eggs

Flour

Breadcrumbs

Vegetable oil to fry

6 toothpicks

The day before making mix chopped parsley with softened butter, salt and pepper and leave in the freezing section of the fridge for 24 hours. Remove the first joint of the wing and flatten the chicken breast with a meat hammer or the flat of your hand, skinned side down. Place a cube of butter on the chicken flesh. Roll the chicken breast into an oval shape around the butter, secure with a toothpick. Season with salt and pepper and dip in the flour and then in the egg and breadcrumbs.

Either deep fry in oil until golden brown and cooked through, or fry until golden and finish the cooking with 2 minutes in the microwave. Serve with straw potatoes and green peas.

1

2

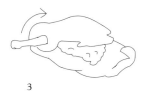
3

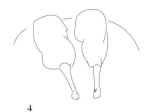
4

Tziplonik Tabaka
(Tabaka chicken)

Ingredients

6 poussin (small chickens)

3 tbs plain yogurt

3 tbs double cream

Salt and pepper

750 g / 1 1/2 lb clarified butter

Spatchcock the poussin by cutting down the backbone and pressing flat on a wooden board. Make two holes on the breast and leg and thread the bones through them to hold in place.

Mix the yogurt with the cream, salt and pepper and spread this over the birds. Leave to stand in the fridge for about 2 hours.

Melt the butter in a large heavy frying pan and fry gently, with a weight on each one to keep flat, until browned, turn and fry the other side still with the weight on top until cooked through.

Kuritza Sous Satsivi
(Chicken with satsivi sauce)

Ingredients

6 chicken breasts with skin and
bones removed
3 tbs butter
1 tbs corn oil
Salt and pepper to taste

Sauce

7 tbs butter
1 cups ground walnuts
2 cups / 400g / 14 oz finely
chopped onions
2 tbs wholewheat flour
4 egg yolks
1 tsp crushed garlic
1/2 cups vinegar
1 tsp dill weed
Pinch of ground cloves
1/2 tsp ground cinnamon
1/2 tsp saffron
Pinch ground bay leaf
Pinch cayenne pepper
Salt to taste
1 cup chicken stock

Melt the butter and oil in a frying pan large enough to take the chicken in a single layer. Brown the breasts on all sides and reduce the heat. Sprinkle on salt and pepper, cover the pan and cook slowly for about 20 minutes. Keep warm.

Sauce

Melt the butter in a small saucepan, add the onion and garlic and cook until golden brown. Sprinkle on the flour and add chicken stock. Cook slowly for about 3 minutes stirring with a wooden spoon. Reduce the heat to the lowest flame and add vinegar, cloves, cinnamon, cayenne, saffron, bay leaf, salt and walnuts. Put the saucepan in a bain Marie or a double saucepan, beat in the egg yolks and continue stirring for about a minute. The sauce must not come to the boil. Remove from the heat immediately and pour over the chicken breasts. Serve with straw potatoes.

(Satsivi is a sauce which can be served either hot or cold. Use it with vegetables, fish or poultry. In El Cosaco we serve it with turkey breasts.)

Poszharskii Kotlety

(Chicken or game croquettes)

Ingredients

3/4 k / 1 1/4 lb minced partridge
or pheasant breast

1/4 k / 8 oz minced chicken or veal

1/2 cup / 4 fl oz cream

3 slices white bread crust removed

1 egg yolk

1 tbs vodka

1 tsp salt

1/2 tsp white pepper

10 tbs butter

1 tbs vegetable oil

Breadcrumbs

Soak bread in the cream for a few minutes. Squeeze out excess moisture. Mix together the bread, egg yolk, vodka, salt and pepper and beat well with a wooden spoon. Gradually beat in the minced meats with four tablespoons of melted butter. Continue beating for 5 minutes until a light mass has formed.

With wet hand, mould the croquettes into oval shapes pressing them down lightly. They should measure about 2 cms/1 in thick. by 4 or 5 cms/2-2 1/2 inches wide. Dip in breadcrumbs and fry croquettes in clarified butter mixed with the vegetable oil on a fairly low heat for about 5 mins each side. They should remain rounded and juicy. (A colourless juice should come out when they are pricked with a fork.)

Serve with fried potatoes and mushrooms sautéed in sour cream.

Induik c Suchonami Fruktami
(Turkey with dried fruit)

Ingredients

1 cup sour cream

2 k / 4 1/2 lb turkey meat

1 large chopped onion

1/2 cup / 100 g / 4 oz raisins

1 cup / 200 g / 8 oz dried apricots sliced

1 cup chicken or turkey stock

1/4 cup / 50 g / 2 oz barberries

(these can be found in Iranian

shops)

4 tbs butter

1/2 tsp salt

1/4 tsp white pepper

Chop turkey meat into medium sized chunks. Sprinkle on salt and pepper and rub in the sour cream. Leave to rest in the fridge for about one hour. Melt the butter in a large frying pan and seal the chunks of turkey meat in the fat, add the onion and continue until golden brown. When onions are soft add the stock and other ingredients. Cover the pan and cook slowly for about 20 minutes. Serve with boiled rice.

Fazan po Ruski
(Russian pheasant)

Ingredients

3 pheasants halved lengthwise

3 sliced carrots

2 small turnips

2 tomatoes

2 onions

Sprig of fresh thyme

Bundle of celery and parsley

Bay leaf

1 glass brandy

1 glass vodka

1 cup / 225 ml / 8 fl oz chicken stock

1 tsp salt

1/2 tsp pepper

Flour

Butter and vegetable oil to fry

1/2 k / 1 lb fresh oyster mushrooms

Fry gently the carrots, turnips, celery and parsley, tomatoes, thyme, onions and bay leaf until soft. Sprinkle salt and pepper on the pheasants, flour them lightly and sauté until golden. Pour on brandy and vodka and flame. Add the softened vegetables with the stock. Cook in a lidded earthenware casserole either in the oven or over a low flame. The cooking time will vary according to the age and toughness of the birds, usually 1-1 1/2 hours. Before serving press the vegetables and sauce through a sieve and add the mushrooms previously sautéed in butter. Serve with steamed potatoes sprinkled with dill weed.

Kuropatki v Smetanie
(Partridge with cream)

Ingredients

3 partridge

20 crushed juniper berries

3 tbs sour cream

3/4 cup butter

2 tbs chopped parsley

Salt and pepper to taste

Pre-heat oven to 200C/400F Gas 6. Wash and dry the partridge well inside and out. Sprinkle salt and pepper on the skin and into the cavities and divide the juniper berries between the three birds. Melt the butter in a cast iron casserole and brown the birds until golden brown. (10 minutes approximately). Cover and cook in the oven for 20 to 25 minutes. Remove the lid and glaze each one with a spoonful of sour cream. Reduce the oven temperature to 180C/350F, Gas 4 and cook for a further 15 minutes or until the birds are brown and tender. Sprinkle the chopped parsley over the birds and serve with braised red cabbage and steamed potatoes.

Zaiats v Smetanie
(Hare with cream)

Ingredients

1 hare (approx 2 kilos/4 1/2 lb)

1/2 cup butter

2 carrots

1 small turnip

1 medium onion

2 cups beef stock

10 black peppercorns

6 juniper berries

2 bay leaves

1 1/2 cups sour cream

Salt to taste

Wash the hare and cover with tepid water. Leave the hare to soak for about 1 hour. Dry with paper towels and chop into serving sized pieces. Melt the butter and brown the pieces of hare for about 5 minutes each side. Cut the carrot, turnip and onion into 1 cm/1/2 inch slices. Place the hare in a cast iron casserole with the vegetables and the spices tied in a muslin bag. Sprinkle over the salt and the stock. Cover and bring to the boil over high heat then lower to the lowest flame and simmer for 30-40 minutes. Preheat the oven to 175C/325F Gas 3. Separate the hare from the liquid and vegetables and place in an oven proof casserole. Discard the bag of spices and sieve the vegetables and stock. Mix the sieved sauce with the sour cream. Add a little salt if necessary and nap the hare with it. Place in the oven and continue cooking for about 20 minutes or until tender. Serve with sautéed cabbage, steamed potatoes and slices of beetroot.

Meat

As I mentioned in an earlier chapter, food in Russia varies widely from north to south, and with meat this difference becomes even more defined. Northerners stew their meat with thick sauces sometimes lightened with sour cream. Many head of cattle were slaughtered in the autumn to be pickled, dried or smoked to keep them through the long cold winters, and since time immemorial Siberia has made use of natural deep freezes.

One very typical dish is "Siberian pelmeni". Pelmeni are similar to ravioli and the Siberians used to make them in vast quantities at the beginning of the Autumn. They were then put into jute sacks and put outside in the garden where they froze in a matter of hours. During the winter months an imaginative housewife used them in many forms — in soups, with onions or in different sauces. The Chinese probably introduced pelmeni into Russia and they quickly spread throughout the country.

The most common meats in Northern Russia are beef, veal, pork, game and even bear; further south they eat more lamb and chicken, and in the predominantly Moslem regions pork is rarely seen. In more southerly regions, where fruit is grown in abundance, meat dishes are often flavoured with lemons, prunes, raisins and nuts. But what all Russians seem to have in common is their refusal to eat any under-cooked meat. So forget the idea of asking for a rare steak anywhere in Russia.

Escallops of veal Skobelev were created in honour of Mijail Skobelev, a brilliant army officer who became a general when he was only thirty, and in 1873 captured Khiva and Turkistan for the Russian crown. He was a man of refined tastes, who had a white uniform designed for himself and always rode white horses. In between fighting battles he spent his time in the company of beautiful women, drinking vodka, eating good food, always accompanied by gypsy music; he met his death eating and drinking in a house of doubtful repute. It is thus appropriate that the dish created in his honour is very refined – and white.

The recipes for beef Strogonov and beef Woronov were invented by French chefs who worked for noble families in Russia. Apparently Count Strogonov, who was a great shot, came home from a shooting party one day with

more guests than were expected for dinner. His chef had planned to serve them tournedos, but when he was told of the increase in numbers, he decided to make the meat go further by cutting it into fingers and serving it in a sauce which he invented for the occasion. He named the dish after his employer and within a short time its fame and popularity had spread even beyond the Russian borders. Beef Woronov took its name from a famous professor of endocrinology of the same name.

Many countries use minced meat in their cooking, and most of them eat some form of hamburger. In Russia these are known as "koteletki" and "bitki" which, along with borscht, are almost the national dishes of the country. The main difference between koteletki and bitki is basically in size and shape; the former are larger and oval, while the latter are smaller and round. There are many ways of preparing and cooking them and they can be eaten hot or cold, with or without sauce.

Shashlik, which almost certainly stem from the various kinds of Mediterranean brochettes or kebabs, only differ from them in that the chunks of meat or fish are usually larger; every southern region has its own variation on the same theme. In general, the marinades contain fewer spices and more fresh ingredients, such as lemon and herbs, than the Mediterranean brochettes. Shashlik are usually served with white rice, grilled tomatoes and a green salad, while in Georgia they are sometimes accompanied by a plum sauce called "tkemali".

Shashlik are grilled over charcoal or wood —experts say that the best are the ones cooked on grape vine cuttings— over which dried aromatic herbs are thrown. Fillet steak shashlik varies from other ones in that it has a marinating time of only around 10 minutes and, so the blood stays in the meat, salt is only added just before serving.

One popular minced meat dish is "golubtzi" or stuffed cabbage rolls. They are believed to be of Byzantine origin, and each region has its own way of cooking them. In the south the stuffing contains finely minced lamb and veal with pine nuts, raisins and spices and the sauce is based on tomato or yogurt. While further north they are made from minced veal and pork, and the sauce is either a Béchamel cream sauce or a tomato sauce to which Béchamel and cream have been added. The recipe I have included is a northern one.

I have also added two typical Easter dishes: baked ham and stuffed lamb.

Tiliatina Skobelev
(Veal escallops with mushroom sauce)

Ingredients

2 finely chopped onions

6 tbs butter

3/4 k / 1 1/2 lb white mushroom
finely sliced

1 k / 2 1/4 lbs thin veal escallops

Salt and white pepper to taste

2 tbs flour

1 cups sour cream

1 cup veal stock

1/4 cup dry white wine

Melt 2 tbs butter in a frying pan and fry the onions until soft. Add the mushrooms and continue cooking, stirring occasionally, until the moisture has evaporated and put to one side.

Trim veal escallops and beat out with a meat hammer until very thin. Cut into 2 cm/1 inch by 5 cm/ 3 inch strips and sprinkle with salt and pepper. Melt two more tbs butter in the frying pan and gently fry the veal strips.

Put the flour in a small saucepan and brown it slightly, stirring all the time, before adding the remaining butter and continue stirring with a wooden spoon. Remove from the heat and gradually add the sour cream mixed with the veal stock. Return to the heat and continue stirring until thickened. Stir the onions and mushroom into the sauce. Add the veal and cook for another 10 minutes over a low heat, stirring occasionally. Add the wine and correct the seasoning. Serve with straw potatoes.

Boeuf Strogonoff
Beef Strogonov

Boeuf Strogonoff
(Beef Strogonov)

Ingredients

1 k / 2 1/4 lb fillet steak

2 large onions

1/4 k / 8 oz finely sliced mushrooms

5 tbs butter

1/4 tsp tabasco

1 tbs HP sauce

1/2 tsp salt

1/4 tsp pepper

2 small glasses vodka

1/2 cup white sauce

1 1/2 cups sour cream

Flour to dredge the meat

Cut fillet steak into long thin strips and dredge with flour. Slice the onions into fine slices and soften in 2 tbs butter, add mushrooms and continue cooking until soft.

Melt the remaining butter in a second pan and sauté the meat over a high heat, pour over the vodka and flame. Add remaining ingredients, mix well and continue cooking over a low heat until thickened slightly. Serve with boiled rice or straw potatoes.

189

Golubtzi
Stuffed cabbage leaves

Golubtzi
(Stuffed cabbage leaves)

Ingredients

1 large cabbage

750g / 1 lb 6 oz minced beef or veal

250 g / 8 oz minced pork and bacon

1 cup cooked rice

1/2 cup chopped onion

2 tbs butter

1 tsp salt

1/4 tsp ground white pepper

1 cup stock

Sauce

1 cup beef stock

1 cup cream

1/2 cup tomato sauce

1/2 cup white sauce

Blanch whole cabbage in a large saucepan of salted water for about 10 minutes until it begins to soften. Remove from the heat and cool in cold water. Remove the leaves, one by one, cutting out the hard core.

Fry the onion in the butter and mix in remaining ingredients. Place a heaped tablespoon of the filling on each cabbage leaf and roll until all the filling is used up. Place the remaining cabbage leaves on the bottom of a wide pan and arrange the cabbage rolls in circles on top. Pour the stock over them, cover and cook over a low heat for 45 minutes. Mix the sauce ingredients and pour over the cabbage rolls. Cook for 5 minutes.

Boeuf Woronoff
(Beef Woronov)

Ingredients

12 thin fillet steak medallions

1 cup sliced pickled cucumber

1/2 cup «Café de Paris» butter

1 1/2 cups sour cream

1 tsp salt

1/2 tsp pepper

1 tsp Worcester sauce

1 tsp HP sauce

Cafe de Paris butter

1 k / 2 1/4 lb butter

1 tbs tomato ketchup

1 tbs mustard

1 tbs capers

1 tbs chopped parsley

1 tbs chopped spring onion (scallion)

1/2 tbs dillweed

1 clove garlic

4 anchovy fillets

1 tbs brandy

1 tbs vodka

1/2 tbs Worcester sauce

1/2 tsp paprika

1 strip lemon rind

Grated rind 1 orange

1/2 tsp salt

1/4 tsp pepper

6 tarragon leaves

As the most troublesome part of this recipe is making the Café de Paris butter it is worthwhile preparing at least 1/2 k/1 lb at a time and storing them in 4 oz/100g slices wrapped in kitchen foil and stored in the freezer for later use.

Melt the butter in a heavy frying pan, sauté pickled cucumbers, and add the sour cream and sauces, spices and citrus rind. Cook over a low heat until it begins to thicken. Add the steaks and press down into the sauce turning after 2 minutes. Cook a further 3 minutes. Adjust seasoning if necessary. Serve with white rice or straw potatoes.

Bitki o Koteletki
(Russian style hamburgers)

Ingredients

1 k / 2 1/4 lb minced beef or
half beef and half pork
1 cup soaked white breadcrumbs
2 eggs
1/2 tsp pepper
1 tsp salt
2 tbs finely chopped softened onions
Flour or breadcrumbs to coat
2 tbs vegetable oil
2 tbs butter

Beat the eggs into the squeezed white breadcrumbs and add the salt, pepper and minced meat. Beat well and shape into bitkis or hamburger shapes and dredge with flour or breadcrumbs. Fry over a moderate heat in the oil and butter turning occasionally until they are golden brown. They can be eaten as they are, garnished with pickled cucumbers, tomato or onion sauce.

Onion sauce

2 finely sliced large onions
1/2 litre / 1 pint white sauce
1 tsp HP sauce
2 tbs butter

Melt the onions in the butter until very soft. Stir in the white sauce and HP sauce. Arrange the bitkis in a shallow heat proof dish and pour the sauce over them. Grill until golden brown.

Zarkoi iz Gaviadini
(Russian style braised beef)

Ingredients

1 1/2 k / 3 lb stewing beef cut
into chunks

1/2 k / 1 lb diced panceta or bacon

1 glass vodka

4 carrots

3 small turnips

6 shallots

1 sprig of tarragon

1 cup dried mushrooms (soaked)

4 tbs vegetable oil

1 cups sour cream

1/2 tsp pepper

6 medium-sized potatoes

2 tsp chopped parsley

Soak the dried mushroom in warm water for several hours. Cut into slices and strain any grit out of the liquid.

Heat the oil in a heavy pan and sauté the meat and panceta until lightly browned. Pour in the vodka and flame, add pepper (it probably will not need salt as the panceta is salted, but add after cooking if necessary). Add the sliced carrots and turnips, whole shallots, tarragon and the mushrooms and 1 cup of strained mushroom liquid. Cover and cook over a very low heat, or in the oven for about 2 hours. When nearly cooked place the potatoes on top of the meat so they cook in the steam. Just before serving remove potatoes to a plate and stir in the sour cream. Served the meat, surrounded by the potatoes and sprinkled with parsley.

Srazi
(Meat rolls)

Ingredients

12 small thin beef steaks

2 cups cooked buckwheat or rice

1/2 cup finely chopped onion

1/2 cup chopped mushroom

1 cup tomato sauce

1 cup beef stock

3 tbs butter

1 tsp salt

1/2 tsp pepper

2 bay leaves

Beat out the steaks with a meat mallet. Melt half the butter and fry the onions. Mix the buckwheat (recipe page 132) or the rice with the mushrooms and onions, season well. Divide the mixture into small piles on each steak. Roll up and tie with fine string or cotton. Brown in a pan with the remaining butter, pour the tomato sauce and the stock over the rolls adding the bay leaf. Cover and simmer slowly for about 1 hour. Serve with vegetables.

Shashlik iz Barachka
Lamb kebabs

Shashlik iz Barachka
(Lamb kebabs)

Ingredients

1 1/2 k / 3 1/2 lb leg or fillet
of lamb boned and cut into
2 cm / 1 inch dice

2 chopped onions

Juice 1 lemon

2 tsp olive oil

1 tsp salt

1/4 tsp pepper

6 rashers bacon in 2 cm / 1 in squares

3 small onions finely sliced

2 green peppers in 2 cm / 1 in squares

6 cherry tomatoes

Marinate the meat with onions, lemon juice, olive oil, salt and pepper in the fridge for several hours. Light the barbecue or grill and thread the kebabs using long metal skewers alternating the diced lamb, bacon, sliced onions, peppers ending with the tomato. Grill over the hot fire turning the skewers from time to time. The cooking time will depend on the heat of the grill. Serve with rice and mixed salad. Tkemali sauce is also very good with these kebabs.

Liulia Kebab
(Caucasian minced meat kebabs)

Ingredients

1 1/2 k / 3 1/2 lbs minced lamb
with some of its fat

1/2 cup finely chopped onion

1 tsp salt

1/2 tsp pepper

2 tbs finely chopped mint

6 long metal skewers

Mix all the ingredients together and beat well with a wooden spoon. Divide the meat into 6 portions and with wet hands form the meat into sausage shapes around each kebab. Cook on the barbecue on under the grill. Serve with pickled onions and lettuce and tomato salad.

Baranina c Chernoslivomi
(Georgian braised lamb with prunes)

Ingredients

1 3/4 k / 4 lbs leg of lamb
cut into 5 cm / 2 inch chunks
4 tbs vegetable oil
3 cups prunes
1 large finely chopped onions
1 cups tomato pasata (fresh
tomato sauce)
2 tbs flour
2 tbs sugar
1/4 cup vinegar
1/2 tsp ground cinnamon
Pinch ground clove
1 tsp salt
1/2 tsp ground black pepper
2 cups lamb stock from bones

Sprinkle meat with salt and pepper. Heat the oil in a casserole and brown the meat, add onion and continue cooking until golden. Pour over the tomato, flour and stock stirring over the heat until thickened slightly. Cover with a lid and simmer slowly for about 20 minutes. Add the sugar, vinegar, cinnamon, cloves and prunes. Continue cooking for 20 minutes longer or until the meat is tender. Served with white rice and glazed carrots.

Kabiga c Garnirom
po Kazanski
Kazan rack of lamb

Kabiga c Garnirom po Kazanski
(Kazan rack of lamb)

Ingredients

2 tbs olive oil

6 cloves finely chopped garlic

3 tsp chopped parsley

Salt and freshly ground black pepper

1 rack of lamb 1.8 k/ 4 lbs

Sauce

2 carrots

2 medium onions

1 stick celery

1 small turnip

Bunch thyme, bay and rosemary

Salt and pepper to taste

1 1/2 cups lamb stock from bones

If not already boned, ask the butcher to do it for you, leaving about 8 cms / 3 inches of the rib bones. Brown the garlic in a little oil. Rub the surface of the meat with the garlic, parsley and black pepper. Roll the meat up to the bones and tie with string. Make a bed of the vegetables and herbs and place the meat on top. Put into a pre-heated oven (200C/400F) until it begins to brown. Sprinkle with salt and reduce the oven temperature to 175C/350F). The meat is done when the juice is clear and with no sign of blood (about 25 minutes after adding the salt is usually sufficient). Press the vegetables into a small saucepan through a conical sieve and dilute with the stock. Reduce slightly over a low heat until it begins to thicken. Cut between each chop and decorate the bones with cutlet frills. Form into a rack again and place on a long platter. Serve with straw potatoes and grilled tomatoes. Serve the gravy separately.

Pochki po Ruski
(Kidneys a la russe)

Ingredients

1 1/2 k/ 3 1/2 lbs veal kidneys

2 cups milk

1 tsp salt

8 tbs butter

6 large potatoes cut in thick slices

2 finely sliced carrots

2 finely sliced onions

2 tbs chopped parsley

2 pickled cucumbers

2 tbs tomato pasata (fresh tomato sauce)

1 clove crushed garlic

Remove the fat from the kidneys and wash in cold water. Cut into two and remove the core. Leave to soak in the milk for about 1 hour. Cut the kidneys into fine slices and sprinkle with the salt. Melt half the butter in a frying pan and fry half the kidneys for 2 minutes on each side. Remove and leave to one side, fry the remaining kidneys.

Return the kidneys into a heavy casserole. Melt 2 tbs butter in the frying pan and fry the onions and carrots for 2 minutes. Add the parsley and salt. Remove to a plate. Melt the remaining butter in the frying pan and fry the potatoes, shaking the pan occasionally, until they begin to brown . Arrange the potatoes on top of the kidneys, with the carrots and onions on top.

In a small saucepan brown the flour, add the butter and gradually mix 2 cups of the stock stirring all the time. Add the bay leaf and the peppercorns and simmer for about 3 minutes.

Sauce

2 tbs flour

4 tbs butter

3 cups chicken stock

1 bay leaf

6 grains black peppercorns

Pour the sauce over the vegetables and kidneys, cover and simmer over a low heat for 30 minutes. If it dries out too much add a little more stock.

Slice the pickled cucumbers lengthwise and add to the kidneys along with the garlic and tomato sauce. Bring back to the boil and remove from the heat immediately. Serve very hot.

 Puddings and Desserts

All Russians, whether from the North or South, love sweets. Ice creams are sold on street corners throughout Russia in winter as well as summer.

Fruit is plentiful in the short hot summers, but it has to be preserved for the long winter months. It can be dried in the sun, preserved in syrup or in granulated sugar in large jars. Fresh apples and pears used to be stored in the cellar on straw; syrup was made from berries and pomegranates to be used later in the year either diluted as refreshing drinks or to add to ice cream; plums and cherries were used to flavour brandy or vodka.

The making of jams and jellies to eat in the winter and cooked in copper pans over a slow heat were a traditional ritual. Other fruit was sprinkled with sugar, covered with a fine muslin to protect it from birds and insects, and left in the sun until it was almost dry.

In winter the preserved fruits were used sparingly as flavourings for desserts which were based on starches like tapioca, corn meal, buckwheat or wheat meal cooked with milk, lightened with egg white or whipped cream and added to the fruit. One of the most popular of this kind of dessert is Gurievskaia Kasha which is reputed to have been invented by Count Dimitri Alexandrovich Guriev to commemorate the Russian victory over Napoleon although I doubt very much whether this gentleman ever set foot inside a kitchen and he most probably instructed his chef to concoct something to suit Russian tastes. It is not an easy dish to prepare, and as far as I am concerned it is one of those best put in the "acquired taste from childhood memories" category.

Another very popular dessert is "kisel" which is mentioned in several ancient fairy stories. Basically kisel is a fruit cream with the consistency of a custard thickened with either potato or corn flour. Any preserved fruit, fruit syrup or jelly can be used and red or white wine, honey or milk is sometimes added.

The recipe for lemon mousse is an adaptation of an ancient Russian recipe and is quite difficult to prepare because to one must begin with a "kaimak", kind of homemade condensed milk.

The story behind Charlotte Russe is a strange one. Many people believe it was originally French because Charlotte is not a Russian name. It probably originated with an old Russian recipe which the great French chef Antoine Careme enjoyed when he came to work for the Imperial Family. He added his own refinements and took it back with him to France where it became popular as Charlotte Russe and has today become a classic of French cuisine.

My father used to tell me how at the end of every winter they used to cut enormous blocks of ice from the river to store in underground caves and cellars so that they could make ice cream in the summer. I also remember him saying that when their country house was full of guests in the summer they never once repeated a dessert throughout the entire season.

Ruski Chai
Russian Tea

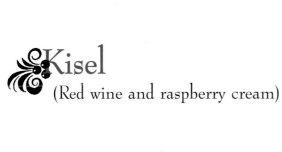

Kisel
(Red wine and raspberry cream)

Ingredients

1/2 litres / 1 pint water

1/4 l / 1/2 pint red wine

1 jar red currant jelly

4 tbs corn flour

A few cloves

1 cup double cream

A little sugar to taste

Combine all the ingredients, except the cream, and stir with a wooden spoon over a medium heat. When it has thickened remove the cloves and pour into individual sundae glasses and leave stand. When cold pour a layer of thick cream over the top.

Compot iz Cherechni
(Cherry compote)

Ingredients

1 k / 2 1/4 lb stoned cherries

8 tbs sugar

Rind from one lemon

1 cups water with juice of lemon

1/4 tsp cinnamon and nutmeg
mixed together

Cream

Poach the fruit with the flavourings over a slow heat for about 15 minutes. Chill the compote and serve the cream separately.

Vareniki c Vichnamy
(Cherry dumplings)

Pastry

1/2 k / 1 lb flour

1 egg

1/2 tsp salt

1 tbs vegetable oil

Water to bind

Filling

3/4 k / 1 3/4 lb stoned and
poached fresh or tinned cherries

Double cream

Make the pastry by kneading together all the ingredients. Cover with clingwrap and leave to rest in the fridge for about 1/2 hour.

Roll out the pastry until very thin on a floured marble slab or in a pasta machine until the thickness of the pasta for ravioli. Cut into circles and fill each one with 2 or 3 cherries. Seal the edges with a little water and press together with a fork.

Poach for about 5 minutes in a large pan of boiling water. Remove with a skimmer and serve with cream and sugar separately.

# Cirniki
(Cheese pancakes)

Ingredients

500 g / 1 lb curd cheese

1/2 cup flour

3 eggs

1/4 cup sugar

Vanilla essence

Butter and vegetable oil to fry

2 cups cream

Jam or fruit syrup to taste

Icing sugar

Beat the eggs with the sugar. Add the flour, curd cheese and vanilla. Knead well. Place the dough on a sheet of floured grease proof paper. Sprinkle on the remaining flour and cover with another sheet of paper. Roll out the dough to the thickness of about 1 cm/1/2 inch. Remove the paper and cut into circles of about 6 or 7 cm / 3 inches. Heat the butter and oil and fry the pancakes until they are browned on both sides. Sprinkle with icing sugar and serve with jam and cream separately.

Sambuk iz Apricosa
(Apricot custards)

Ingredients

1/2 cup water

Rind of 1 lemon

1/2 k apricots

1 tbs lemon juice

1 cup sugar

2 Egg whites

5 sheets gelatine or 1 pkt. lemon
jelly (in which case omit lemon juice)

Stone the apricots. Poach in the water with lemon rind. Remove the lemon rind and purée the fruit. Chill.

Whip the egg whites and beat in the sugar and apricot purée until you have a soufflé consistency. Soften the gelatine in a little warm water and gradually beat into the fruit purée.

Pour the mixture into individual dishes and chill until set. Dip the dishes into warm water and turn out on to serving plates. Decorate each one with a little whipped cream and a few slices of fresh apricot.

Klubnika Romanoff
Strawberries Romanov

Klubnika Romanoff
(Strawberries Romanov)

Ingredients

3/4 / 2 lb strawberries

1/2 cup sugar

2 cups whipped cream

2 cups vanilla ice cream

3 tbs orange liqueur

Slice strawberries and sprinkle with sugar. Leave to rest a few hours in the fridge. Mix the whipped cream with ice cream and add the liqueur. Put in the freezing compartment for one hour. Serve in individual glasses. Put the strawberries in first and cover with the ice cream mixture. Decorate with a few sliced strawberries.

Alexanderski Tort
(Alexander cake)

Ingredients

1/4k / 1/2 lb very cold butter

3 cups flour

2 tbs sugar

1 egg

1 cup raspberries

1/2 cup raspberry jam

2 cups icing sugar

2 tsp lemon juice

1/4 cup water

Dice the very cold butter and mix together the butter, flour and the sugar until they resemble coarse breadcrumbs. Beat the egg and quickly mix into the dough and shape into a ball. Wrap in grease proof paper and chill in the fridge for about an hour.

Blend the raspberries with the raspberry jam. Heat the oven to 250C / 500F. Cut the dough into two halves and roll each one out between sheets of floured grease proof paper. Cut into rectangles of 20 cm by 15 cm / 8 in x 6 in. Remove excess flour and paint surface with melted butter. Cook on a tray in the oven for about 20 minutes. They should not brown. Remove from the oven and immediately cover with the raspberry jam and cover with the other sheet of pastry. Make an icing by mixing the icing sugar with the water and lemon juice and pour on the pastry. Leave to set.

Cut into 4 cm slices with a sharp knife, and then cut again diagonally to form diamond shapes.

Jabloki c Slivcami
(Baked apples with cream)

Ingredients

3 tbs sugar

3 tbs butter

6 cooking apples

1 cup sugar

1/4 l / 1/2 pt cream

Grated rind 1 lemon

2 tbs apricot jam

5 egg yolks

Core the apples. Mix the 3 tbs sugar with the butter and stuff into the centre of each apple. Bake over a medium heat, remove from the oven when half cooked.

Meanwhile beat the egg yolks with the 1 cup sugar and add the cream, lemon rind and jam. Pour this over the apples and return to the oven to finish cooking, about 20 minutes. These can be eaten either hot or cold.

221

Tort Tatiana
Tatiana mousse cake

Tort Tatiana
(Tatiana mousse cake)

Ingredients

16 Nice biscuits

50 g / 2 oz melted butter

4 eggs (separated)

6 sheets fine gelatine

1/2 cup hot water

1/2 cup sugar

Small glass brandy

2 cups whipped cream

150 g / 6 oz block good quality chocolate

Make biscuit crust by crushing the biscuits to fine crumbs. Mix in melted butter and press into the base of a cake tin with the back of a spoon or by hand.

Soak the gelatine with the water. Melt the chocolate over hot water and immediately remove from the heat. Beat egg yolks with the sugar until fluffy and gradually mix into the melted chocolate with the brandy. Put in the fridge to chill.

Whip the cream until it holds its shape but not too stiff. Whip egg whites until stiff. Fold the cream and then egg whites into the chocolate mixture and pour over the biscuit crust. Chill for a couple of hours and decorate with whipped cream and a few walnuts.

Cirnik c Vichniami
(Cherry cheesecake)

Ingredients

1/2 l / 3/4 pt. cream

Juice 1/2 lemon

1 tub Quark

6 sheets fine gelatine

1/4 cup water

3/4 cup sugar

Few drops vanilla essence

1 k / 2 lb tin cherries

1 glass kirsch

2 tbs sugar

10 Nice biscuits

50 g / 2 oz melted butter

Crush the biscuits to fine crumbs. Mix with melted butter and press into the base of cake tin.

Whip the cream with the sugar. Soften the gelatine in the water and melt without boiling. Mix the quark with lemon juice, vanilla, gelatine and cream. Pour on to the biscuit crust. Dissolve 2 tbs sugar in the kirsch and dip the cherries into this syrup. Pour over the cheese mixture and refrigerate for a couple of hours.

Limonei Mous
(Lemon mousse)

Ingredients

Juice 3 lemons

3 eggs (separated)

1 1/2 tin condensed milk

1 pkt powdered gelatine

4 cups whipped cream

Cook the condensed milk, lemon juice, beaten egg yolks and the gelatine in a bowl over a pan of hot water, stirring all the time until it begins to thicken. Cool until it reaches room temperature. Fold in the stiffly beaten egg whites and whipped cream. Pour into individual glasses and chill for 2 hours. Serve with biscuits.

Cirnik
(Cheesecake)

Ingredients

1/2 k /1 lb curd cheese

3 large eggs

100 g / 4 oz butter

10 glacé cherries (chopped)

50 g / 2 oz currants

350 g tin condensed milk

1 glass milk

3 tbs corn flour

Grated rind 1 lemon

1/2 k / 1 lbs puff or short crust

pastry

Roll out the pastry and line a high-sided cake tin. Beat the eggs and add the melted butter. Whip all the ingredients, including the eggs and butter, with an electric mixer. Fill the cake tin. Cook in a medium oven for about 35 minutes. Serve either warm or cold.

Ponchiki

(Jam fritters)

Ingredients
(for 15 fritters)

1 tbs baker's yeast

2 tbs tepid water

1/4 cup sugar

2 egg yolks

3/4 cup tepid milk

1 3/4 cups flour

1/4 tsp salt

1 tbs rum

1 tsp vanilla essence

1/4 cup melted butter

Butter to grease the dish

1 l vegetable oil to fry

2 tbs icing sugar

Jam

Stir the yeast into 2 tbs warm water with 1/2 tsp sugar and leave to rise for 15 minutes.

Whip the egg yolks with the sugar for 2 minutes until white and fluffy. Pour into the processor, and with the motor running add the milk, flour, salt and yeast. Process at slow speed for 4 minutes. Add the butter, rum, vanilla and jam processing for another 4 minutes. The dough should become elastic but not too soft.

Grease a 3 litre bowl with butter. Shape the dough into a ball and put into the bowl, turn it a few times until it is covered with the butter. Cover with a cloth, cover with a cloth and leave to prove in a warm place for 2 hours.

Punch down the dough and divide into two portions. Roll out half the dough on a marble slab until thin. Cut into 6 cm / 3 inch circles and holding the dough in the palm of the hand place a little jam in the centre of each circle. With the other hand draw up the dough to seal each ponchiki. Place on a greased tray while preparing the remaining ponchiki. Repeat using the remaining dough. This is easier to do if the hands are dry and cleaned of any grease.

Heat the oil in a deep frying pan or electric fryer. Fry 3 or 4 ponchiki at a time for about 2 minutes each side. Remove on drain on a paper towel. Sprinkle with icing sugar.

Charlotka po Ruski
(Charlotte russe)

1st recipe

Ingredients

1 1/2 tbs butter to grease mould

20 cm square tin mould

20 slices white bread

3 eggs

1/2 cup cream

1/2 cup milk

2 tbs sugar

3 cooking apples

1/2 cup raspberry jam

1/2 cup water

1 tsp vanilla extract

6 cubes butter

Preheat the oven to 190 C /375 F. Grease the mould with butter. Remove the crust from the bread and lightly toast the slices.

Beat the eggs with the sugar until light and fluffy. Mix together the milk, cream and vanilla extract and gradually mix into the beaten eggs. Peel and finely slice the apples. Mix the jam with the water and rum.

Soak 4 slices of bread in the egg and milk mixture and line the base of the mould. Then dip 6 more slices of bread into the mixture and use to line the sides of the mould. Put 1/3 of the apples on the bread and cover with half the jam and another third of the apples. Dip four more slices of bread into the egg and cream mixture and place over the apples, repeat with the jam and the remaining apples, finish with a layer of bread, cutting the edges to fit the tin. Pour remaining cream mixture over the top and put a few cubes of butter on the top. Place in the oven for about 30 minutes or until a knife comes out clean. Turn out on to a shallow dish

Gogol-Mogol sauce

4 egg yolks

4 tbs sugar

1 tsp rum

1/2 tsp vanilla extract

2 stiffly beaten egg white

or tray while still warm. Spread a layer of raspberry jam on the top. Serve warm accompanied by Gogol-mogol sauce.

Gogol-Mogol sauce

Beat the egg yolks with the sugar until pale and fluffy. Add the rum and vanilla and continue beating. Fold in the stiffly beaten egg whites.

Charlotka po Ruski

(Charlotte russe)

2nd recipe, for 8 people

Ingredients

1 1/2 tbs butter to grease mould

1 loaf tin mould

3 tbs breadcrumbs

4 large egg yolks

1/2 cup sugar

2 1/2 cups cream

1 tbs rum

8 cups stale white bread diced

1 k / 2 1/4 lb Golden Delicious apples

4 tbs butter cut into dice

4 tbs cherry or raspberry jam

Grease the loaf tin with the butter and sprinkle it with the breadcrumbs. Preheat the oven to 190C / 375 F. Beat the egg yolks at maximum speed with the sugar for about 3 minutes until light and fluffy. Reduce the speed and gradually add the rum and cream.

Peel and finely slice the apples and mix with the diced bread and pour the cream mixture over them. Pour into the loaf tin and put the diced butter on top. Cook for 30-40 minutes in the oven until a knife comes out clean. Cool slightly and turn out of the tin. Cut into slices and decorate each slice with a little jam.

Serve warm with a little cream on the side. (This recipe is delicious but less spectacular than the previous one. It has the advantage that any stale bread can be used.)

230

Sauces

Maionez
(Mayonnaise)

Ingredients

2 egg yolks

2 cups corn or sunflower oil

1 tsp salt

1/4 tsp sugar

juice 1/2 lemon

1/4 tsp white pepper

Beat together the egg yolks with the salt and drop by drop add half the oil, then the sugar, lemon juice and the pepper. Continue beating until all the oil is used.

Sous Tatarski
(Tartar sauce)

Ingredients

2 cups mayonnaise

1/2 cup chopped capers

1 tbs finely chopped spring onions

1 tsp chopped dill (fresh or dried)

Mix all ingredients together.

Rosavei Sous
(Cocktail sauce)

Ingredients

2 cups mayonnaise

2 tbs brandy

3 tsp tomato sauce

1 tsp dried dillweed

Mix all ingredients together.

Sous iz Hrena
(Horseradish sauce)

Ingredients

Recipe 1

1/2 cup grated horseradish
1/2 cup sour cream

Recipe 2

1/2 cup grated horseradish
1/2 cup finely chopped beetroot

Recipe 1

Mix the horseradish with the sour cream.

Recipe 2

Mix the horseradish with the beetroot.

# Sous Bechamel
(White sauce)

Ingredients

3 tbs butter

2 tbs flour

2 cups hot milk

1/2 cup cream

Salt and pepper to taste

Melt the butter in a saucepan over a low heat. Stir in the flour until it forms a paste. Gradually add the warm milk and cream, stirring with a wooden spoon for about 8 minutes until thickened and all taste of raw flour has gone. Season with salt and pepper.

Smetana
(Sour cream)

Ingredients

1/2 litre / 1 3/4 pts cream

1 plain yogurt

juice 1 lemon

If you can't find sour cream on the supermarket shelves, it is easy to make your own. Gradually mix the cream with the yogurt and lemon juice. Leave to stand overnight at room temperature. Beat again before serving.

Sous Tkemali
(Tkemali sauce)

Ingredients

2 cups water

1/2 k / 1 lb prunes

1 clove garlic

3 tsp coriander or parsley

1/2 tsp salt

Pinch cayenne pepper

2 tsp lemon juice

Stone the prunes and cook in the water for about 10 minutes. Add remaining ingredients and process. Return to the saucepan and cook over a low heat for about 5 minutes, stirring all the time.

238

Sous Strogonoff
(Strogonov sauce)

Ingredients

1 cup chopped onions softened
in butter

1 cup cooked sliced mushrooms

1/2 cup white sauce

1 cup sour cream

1 tbs HP sauce

1/2 tbs soy sauce

Mix all the ingredients together and cook over a low heat for a few minutes. Pour over the bitki (recipe page 193) and serve with boiled rice.

Index of recipes